GREAT
IRISH
HEROES

DANNY CONLON AND ALAN BARTER

GREAT IRISH HEROES

MICHAEL COLLINS, BILLY THE KID,
TEDDY ROOSEVELT, NED KELLY: FIFTY TRUE
STORIES OF IRISH MEN AND WOMEN WHO
CHANGED THE WORLD

JOHN BLAKE

Published by John Blake Publishing Ltd,
3 Bramber Court, 2 Bramber Road,
London W14 9PB, England

www.johnblakepublishing.co.uk

First published in paperback in 2003
This edition published in paperback in 2010

ISBN: 978 1 84454 882 8

British Library Cataloguing-in-Publication Data:
A catalogue record for this book is available from the British Library.

Design by www.envydesign.co.uk

Printed in Great Britain by CPI Group (UK) Ltd, Croydon, CR0 4YY

3 5 7 9 10 8 6 4

Papers used by John Blake Publishing are natural, recyclable products made
from wood grown in sustainable forests. The manufacturing processes
conform to the environmental regulations of the country of origin.

This book is published in conjunction with the News of the World. John
Blake Publishing is grateful to the News of the World for supplying all the
images used in this book.

CONTENTS

BRENDAN BRACKEN

The Irishman who helped
Churchill defeat Hitler

Through the darkest days of the Second World War Winston Churchill had a loyal friend perpetually at his side. Irishman Brendan Bracken sustained and guided the great wartime leader safely through a decision-making minefield few mortal minds could cope with. They were so close, Churchill's wife Clemmie wrongly thought Bracken was her husband's secret illegitimate child.

It was a remarkable story of a rebellious lad who once ran wild in the streets of Dublin, making his mother sick with worry. But the scallywag with a mop of red hair that stood out like a halo would not be tamed. He vandalised neighbours' gardens, scrumped apples and threw a schoolfellow into a canal. Misdemeanours were legion as he bordered on total delinquency.

His despairing mother sent him to a Jesuit boarding school at Mungret just before his 15th birthday but he ran away from the continually carping clerics there. Then he was packed off to Australia to stay with his mother's cousin who was a priest in an outback town.

Spirited Bracken became a wild rover – moving between religious houses, teaching and reading incessantly.

The experiences were forming the man who in the future would stand shoulder to shoulder with men who literally ruled the world. His rise would be astonishing.

- He founded the mighty *Financial Times* newspaper empire in London and mixed in high society circles.
- He was pals with publishing magnate Lord Beaverbrook who introduced him to powerful banking figures and told him to prepare for being the next Conservative Prime Minister after Churchill.
- He was Churchill's wartime Minister of Information – the first political spin doctor who some said built his career and huge wealth on blarney and name dropping.
- He never took his seat in the House of Lords as he mischievously said that it was like a morgue.
- He became Viscount Bracken in 1951 and retired from politics through ill health.

Brendan Bracken was born at Templemore, Co Tipperary, in 1901. His father, well-to-do builder Joseph

The Allies' planes during the Battle of Britain, the decisive air battle they won.

Bracken, was a member of the Fenian brotherhood, which was committed to winning Irish independence by force of arms. Joseph died when the lad was three. A few years later the family of six children moved to Dublin. When young Bracken returned from Australia in 1919 he found his mother had remarried and moved to the country.

Rebellion was raging in Ireland and his stepfather Patrick Laffan was sympathetic to the rebels. Bracken was not. So he took a boat to Liverpool in January, 1920 and wangled a teaching job at Liverpool Collegiate College by claiming he was *four* years older than his actual age. He said he was a former head boy at an Australian public school and a graduate of Sydney

The D-day landing, Bracken bolstered Churchill during this

University. Eight months later he turned up at Sedbergh School in Lancashire, and said he was only 16 and had lost both parents in an Australian bush fire. Bracken claimed they had left him money to be educated. He was admitted and in one term won a history prize.

It was an important turn in his life – he now had papers that showed he was an English public-school man. He knew from his understanding of English society that it meant doors would be opened to him.

After several teaching jobs he joined a branch of the League of Nations Union at Bishop Stortford, north of London, and made impressive, passionate pro-Imperialist speeches.

His circle of friends enabled him to move to London and get a job on the *Empire Review* magazine. He met JL Garvin, a former editor of the *Observer*, who introduced him to Churchill. The two men soon aired their shared views, which included a reverence for the past and Conservatism – and many a bottle of superior Cognac and boxes of Cuban cigars.

Bracken organised two unsuccessful parliamentary election campaigns for Churchill. In 1924 Churchill rejoined the Conservative Party, after having switched to the Liberals, was returned to Parliament and became Chancellor of the Exchequer under Prime Minister Stanley Baldwin.

Bracken wrote home to his mother, 'I shall never be so happy as I was last week. Dear Winston has become Chancellor.'

The boy from Tipperary's high-society contacts led him into publishing. At 25 he joined the board of an important London publishing firm, and made a fortune and bought a fine house. He had a butler, cook and chauffeur, and period furniture and works of art.

He enjoyed trips to Venice and a home in the country. It is there that he is said to have met Evelyn Waugh who based the character Rex Mottram in *Brideshead Revisited* on fast-talking Bracken. Mottram could fix anything.

Bracken made quiet trips to Ireland to see his ailing mother who died of cancer in 1928.

When it came to girlfriends, Bracken was choosy. He became a suitor of Penelope Dudley Ward, whose mother Freda was the mistress of the Prince of Wales, later Edward VII, for many years.

In 1929 he became a Conservative Member of Parliament for a London constituency and attached himself to Churchill. He was known as Churchill's disciple. They fought against self-government for India and from 1934 vigorously urged rearmament as Hitler and Nazism set the wheels of military menace in motion.

When Churchill flagged, Bracken's vitality revived him. In 1938 Bracken's house in Westminster became the centre for the fight against appeasement. It was from there that Churchill sallied forth that year to deliver his denunciation of the Munich agreement, about which the then Prime Minister Neville Chamberlain declared, 'This means peace in our time.'

Hitler was largely ignored by the British in the early days
of his leadership.

In Germany, Adolf Hitler had captured the mood of
his nation, promising them vengeance for what they
felt was the way they had been humiliated in the Treaty
of Versailles after their defeat in the First World War.
He promised them that Germany would one day be a
great nation again and rule the world.

Bracken and Churchill watched this unnerving
situation unfold before them and believed this could
only mean one thing – another world war. From
Britain's perspective this was disastrous, but for some
reason the rest of Churchill's countrymen and the
world did not see this emerging threat. Bracken now
took on a key role as Churchill's advisor and confidant.

Winston Churchill and Brendan Bracken during their pre-war campaign, urging Britain to rearm. Both have their trademark cigars.

The great man was now fighting an uphill battle in the government of the day as the official policy seemed to be simply to appease Hitler and his regime. The public and the Chamberlain Government turned against Churchill, branding him and Bracken warmongers.

When, on the fateful day of the outbreak of war in 1939, Churchill became First Lord of the Admiralty, Bracken accompanied him as his first Parliamentary Private Secretary. Bracken famously posed for a picture beside his pal Churchill on the doorstep of his London home before the pair set out to debate Mussolini's invasion of Albania.

In May, 1940, Bracken sat at Winston Churchill's right hand when he became Prime Minister and stood against the Nazi onslaught. This cheeky lad from rural Ireland had grown up to become one of the most powerful men in Britain. He moved into 10 Downing Street, helping to choose the Cabinet and giving guidance to Churchill during the Battle of Britain air onslaught.

Bracken would also help forge a new relationship with the US and help influence American public opinion in favour of them joining the conflict on the side of the Allies. He watched some of the darkest moments as war raged from the skies high above London during the Blitz. And he sat with Churchill for many hours while the D-Day landings were taking place, and also when the destruction of Hitler's tyrannical rule finally came about in the streets of Berlin.

Even though Bracken and Churchill would have

blazing rows and arguments on policy, there was never ill feeling between the two men. The loyalty of the pair never wavered as they guided Britain to the final victory over the Nazi regime. Bracken stood behind Churchill as he saluted massed crowds in London at the end of the war … one of the greatest moments in British history. But when Churchill made a triumphant return to power in 1951 Bracken refused to take any office and retired from politics for good.

Heavy smoker Bracken, a man who had risen to the top of the British establishment, died in 1958 of lung cancer. Ironically he once said, 'I shall die young and be forgotten.' His ashes were scattered on Romney Marshes in Kent. All his private papers were destroyed by his chauffeur under the orders of his will. He did not want details of his career to detract in any way from the recorded feats and speeches of his bosom buddy Churchill.

Churchill's son Randolph was jealous of Bracken's close relationship with his father and said of him, 'He was the fantasist whose fantasies came true.'

Clemmie Churchill blamed him for taking her husband away from her. She complained that she disliked brash young Bracken from the day he was an uninvited guest in her home who slept on her drawing-room sofa. The trouble was that the Irish lad kept his shoes on.

MICHAEL COLLINS

How an assassin's bullet
killed peace

Fearless patriot General Michael Collins was hours away from brokering a civil war peace deal when a sniper's bullet cut him down. He had travelled in secret from Dublin to west Cork to meet anti-Treaty agents of Eamon de Valera.

Collins told Captain John L O'Sullivan, who led the West Cork Flying Column and was a pal from schooldays in Clonakilty, that the killing between former comrades was about to end. O'Sullivan warned Collins that he was in great danger and should have a sizeable army escort. The offer was refused. Collins told him, 'They won't kill me in my own county.'

But on the morning of August 22, 1922, at Beal na mBlath – Galaelic for 'Gap of Flowers' – in west Cork, Collins' small convoy was ambushed and he was killed. To this day it is not known who pulled the trigger that robbed Ireland of one of its greatest leaders – or if he was betrayed.

It meant the pro-Treaty army carried on fighting for another eight months with hundreds of Irish lives lost that might have been saved. The anti-Treaty rebels gave up the armed struggle in April, 1923.

A deeply upset O'Sullivan said later, There were about 100 of us stationed in Bandon the night before I got a request to go to the local Munster Arms. I was shocked to find Michael Collins was there, because communication at the time was so bad we hadn't heard that he was on his way down.

But Collins was not on a social visit to meet with old comrades who had stayed loyal to him. Instead, he said, he was on a mission of peace.

O'Sullivan added, 'He gave me a big welcome and asked how things were progressing.

Then he said to me, "I am down here to finish the war." As far as I could figure out from what he was saying, he was down in Cork to meet someone to try to get the whole thing ended.'

Collins left Bandon the next morning to inspect his troops based around the rolling countryside of Cork and also to try to secure a secret peace deal to end the bloody civil war.

Although Collins had an escort of Free State soldiers with him, most were raw recruits and did not have the local knowledge that O'Sullivan and his men possessed. They probably could have saved his life, but Collins was a warrior who laughed at danger.

Collins in uniform as an army chief.

Tom Barry, a pal of Collins who became IRA Chief of Staff.

But, along with the column of Republicans who lay in wait for Collins at Beal na mBlath, there was also another Republican force that happened to come across the fire fight by chance. When Collins and his Free State convoy came under attack, he leapt out of his car and commanded his troops to stand and fight. Historians believe they could have driven through the ambush to safety – but that was not Collins' way.

As the fire fight raged, Republican forces on a cliff face overlooking the road began to retreat as Collins' men turned machine guns on them. Collins moved further up the road to get a clear view of the attackers as they fled when a single bullet to the head mortally wounded him. It is now thought that it came from the second Republican group that came on the attack by chance as they were returning to their to base.

O'Sullivan, who died in 1990, only heard about Collins' death two days after the ambush because he was travelling on missions through west Cork himself at the time. He said, 'The one thing I'll never forget was the feeling everybody had when they heard of his death. Everybody was shocked, stunned and left in tears. With all his escapes in the past we thought he was invulnerable to any bullet and he had been the one man who could have united this whole country.'

O'Sullivan, who had grown up with Collins, was arrested on several occasions and faced death on a daily basis as a battle-hardened fighter in the War of Independence. He joined Cork guerrilla leader Tom Barry on several raids where the two men became good friends before fighting on opposite sides in the civil war. When hostilities ended, their friendship was rekindled and Barry even confided in a pub that maybe, with hindsight, he might have chosen a different side.

The course of Collins' short life as general was set on July 12, 1921 after a War of Independence truce was signed and de Valera led a delegation to London for exploratory talks with the British Prime Minister, David Lloyd George. The talks broke down over the issue of a united Irish Republic, a concession Lloyd George was not about to give.

In September of that year, de Valera was elected

President of the Irish Republic and he offered to negotiate as representative of a sovereign state. Lloyd George refused. He would allow peace talks only with a view of how Ireland might reconcile their national aspirations within the British Empire. Knowing that neither a Republic nor a united Ireland could be won at such talks, de Valera refused to attend. Instead, he sent Arthur Griffith and Michael Collins to head the Irish delegation. Neither man wanted to go. Collins declared that he was a soldier, not a politician, but the issue went to the Cabinet and was decided by de Valera's casting vote.

The two men were no match for the cunning of Lloyd George. One Irish historian called it the worst single decision of de Valera's life.

Collins and Griffith pressed for a united Ireland. Differences within the Irish delegation added to the difficulty, but Britain's refusal to consider anything less than dominion status, excluding Ulster, created additional conflict.

Michael Collins knew that a Republic that included the North was not possible under the present conditions, but he hoped for a boundary commission that would redraw the border to include much of Catholic Fermanagh and Tyrone in the newly created Free State.

This left the problem of the Oath of Allegiance. A reworded oath might pass a Dail vote, Collins thought, and, though opposed by de Valera, would pave the way for future concessions once a British troop withdrawal was effected. Reluctantly, the delegation signed. Collins knew it would be received badly in Dublin, but he decided that

O'Sullivan, a friend of Collins since school days, who led the West Cork Flying Column.

a step toward Irish independence was preferable to an all-out war that would ensure more bloodshed.

Collins spoke prophetically when, after signing the treaty, he said, 'I tell you, I have signed my death warrant.'

The vote in favour of accepting the treaty was 64 to 57. Two days later, de Valera resigned his presidency and Arthur Griffith was elected in his place. A provisional government was formed in January, 1922. Michael Collins was elected chairman.

Across the country, the IRA split into pro-Treaty or anti-Treaty forces. Many followed Collins, accepting that the Treaty gave the country the freedom to win freedom. Richard Mulcahy, the Minister of Defence, transformed

Michael Collins speaking to pro-Treaty Nationalists in Dublin, April 1922.

these loyal troops into the Free State Army, while the anti-Treaty forces became known as the Irregulars.

Collins made every effort to avoid a civil war. He drafted a new constitution, which he hoped would be acceptable to the Republicans. The rebels had been Collins' comrades-in-arms and he desperately wanted to avoid a tragedy, but his efforts failed. In a move to dislodge Republican troops who had taken over the Four Courts building, on June 28 Collins ordered it to be shelled.

In a controversial move, he armed both pro- and anti-Treaty IRA members in the North to defend the Catholic population but, by resorting to violence against the Treaty terms in the North, he legitimised armed resistance in the South.

On July 6, 1922, the provisional government appointed a council of war and Collins became commander-in-chief of the national army. Opponents of the Treaty rallied to the cause. Fighting broke out in Dublin and Cathal Brugha was killed. The ten-month civil war had begun.

The first phase was bloody and brief. By August, the better-equipped government forces had driven the Irregulars out of the main cities and towns, but the Republicans controlled much of the country area to the south and west.

On August 12, 1922, Arthur Griffith died of a stroke caused by the strain of the Treaty negotiations. Ten days later, though ill with the stomach trouble that had plagued him for several months and suffering from a bad cold, Collins left on his fateful mission to visit troops and attempt to bring about peace.

He set out from Cork in a convoy that passed through Bandon, Clonakilty, and Rosscarbery on its way to Skibbereen. He stopped at Woodfield, and there, in the Four Alls, the pub situated across the road from the house where his mother had been born, he treated his family and escort to the local brew, Clonakilty Wrastler.

On the return trip the convoy again passed through Bandon and on to the Beal na mBlath – the mouth of flowers – ambush. Only Collins was killed.

Collins' men brought his body back to Cork where it was shipped to Dublin. His body lay in state for three days.

The Belfast-born artist Sir John Lavery painted Collins in death, as he had in life. Hundreds of thousands filed past Collins' casket to pay their respects, and even more lined the Dublin streets as the cortege made its way to Glasnevin for the burial.

There have been many famous Irish patriots before him but none conjures up as much emotion and mystery as Collins. In a span of six short years, 32-year-old Collins brought a country from bondage to a position where she could win her freedom.

GREAT IRISH HERO
DE VALERA

De Valera fought and led his nation through one of the most difficult periods in Irish history. He helped to gain attention from the world for the recognition of the Irish State.

NED KELLY

**How the legend of the infamous
outlaw was born amid the grinding
misery of Ireland's famine**

**Legendary 19th-century Irish-Australian outlaw Ned
Kelly – the Robin Hood of his day – has always
been a popular star of the big screen. The film offering
from Hollywood, *The Kelly Gang*, which starred the late
Heath Ledger in the lead role, propelled the infamous
outlaw – who wore iron body armour including a
bucket-like helmet – into the psyche of yet another
generation of filmgoers.**

But his legend would probably never have been born
had it not been for Ireland's Great Hunger. The famine of
the early 1800s, during which a million people died, also
forced another million to flee Ireland in search of a better
life abroad. But thousands, too, were forced into exile as
punishment for wrongdoing – mostly stealing to feed
themselves and their families.

23

Heath Ledger as Ned Kelly.

Ned's father, Tipperaryman John 'Red' Kelly, was one of them. He had stolen two pigs to help feed his parents and siblings. He was arrested, convicted and sentenced to transportation to Australia. After serving a jail sentence there he was freed, but he was a long way from home in a strange, hard land with no possibility of returning to Ireland.

Shortly after his release he met Ellen Quinn, who had emigrated with her family from Ballymena, Co. Antrim, and they married in Melbourne, Victoria, in 1850. They settled in the Victoria countryside and Ned was born there in 1854.

The newest film set Ledger firmly among the new crop of movie stars. Kelly was last portrayed by Rolling Stones frontman Mick Jagger in the film Ned Kelly in 1970, with a dreadful 'Oirish' accent, which the Australian-born Ned

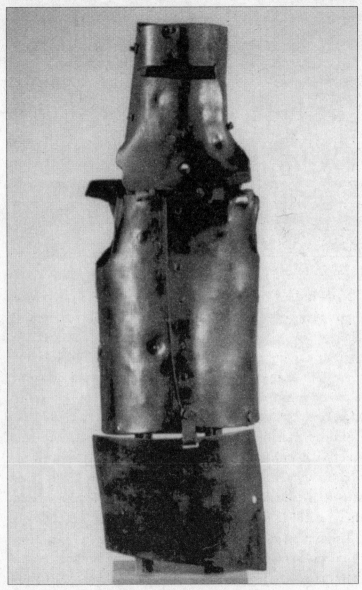

Ned Kelly's armour.

Constable Fitzpatrick.

would never have had. Over 30 years later the film-makers claim to be behind the most authentic rendition. It was written and produced by an Irish-Australian, John Michael McDonagh.

The celluloid pedigree of the outlaw goes back to the beginning of the burgeoning film industry with a silent film in 1906 – just 26 years after Ned's death. Such were the myths and legends that had grown up around this martyr of the common people who stole from the rich and gave to the poor.

Growing up, Ned was to become well known for his defiance and courage. His life was shaped by his strong family ties, the grinding poverty they experienced, the corrupt politics of the time and a wild, rugged country life.

John Kelly died when Ned – the eldest of eight – was just

The Glenrowan Inn where hero Ned Kelly had his final battle with the Victoria state police.

A helmeted Ned Kelly.

A depiction of Ned Kelly on his way to the gallows aged 25.

12 years old. Ned had to help feed his widowed mother, and little brothers and sisters. He became a thief, mostly stealing stock. He was jailed for three years with hard labour for receiving a horse, which he claimed he had not known was stolen.

On his release he returned home, a hardened 19-year-old set for a life of crime not only to feed and care for his own family but also his poor neighbours. So it was that, in the late 1870s, Kelly became a Robin Hood-type bushranger, in what he saw as a fight for justice for poorer people. He was the voice of the disadvantaged.

It was a run-in with a policeman, Constable Alexander Fitzpatrick, in April, 1878 that sent Ned on the run. He maintained that the constable, worse for drink, had attacked one of his sisters. Ned and his mother came to her rescue and Ned shot the man in the wrist. The constable claimed he had visited the Kelly home to 'make an arrest' when Ned and his mother attacked him. He charged them with attempted murder. Mrs Kelly was jailed for three years but Ned fled and a big bounty was put on his head. Ned offered to give himself up for the release of his mother but, when this offer was turned down, he, his brother Dan and several friends formed a gang of bushrangers.

Three policeman were sent to flush out and arrest the two Kelly brothers although contemporary lore has it that they were sent to kill them. However, the Kelly gang caught them off-guard and asked them to surrender. The officers resisted and in the fight which ensued Ned shot them dead.

To the authorities it appeared that the Kelly gang had ambushed and massacred the patrol. The equivalent of a £12,000 reward – a fortune in those days, which would take a tradesman or skilled worker a lifetime to earn – was offered for their capture, dead or alive.

But the gang had the backing of many of their neighbours and poor people throughout the state, who saw them as heroes fighting a corrupt regime. The infamous outlaws went on to rob two banks – in Euroa and Jerilderie

The real Ned Kelly, the bearded hero of the common people.

– which netted them the equivalent of £6,600. They gave much of the money to their impoverished friends. The legend of bushranger Ned Kelly – the Robin Hood of Australia – was born.

And the gang added to their notoriety and mystique by making suits of armour including the famous bucket-like helmets. The iron suits protected them from police pistol and carbine bullets, enabling them to escape without having to kill any of their adversaries. It was part of Ned's efforts to avoid bloodshed and it fed the popular image of his gang as 'brave and bold bushrangers'. At their robberies a defiant Ned also left letters for the state government explaining how he'd been persecuted by the police. Fitzpatrick was labelled a liar and Ned justified his killing of the three policemen as self-defence.

He also wrote actively and bluntly in the name of the poor, in one of these missives stating, 'I have no intention of asking mercy for myself of any mortal man, or apologising, but I wish to give timely warning that if my people do not get justice and those innocents released from prison, I shall be forced to seek revenge of everything of the human race for the future.'

But, the authorities merely vowed to hunt him down. One cold June morning in 1880 Ned fought his final battle at the Glenrowan Inn in Victoria, where police surrounded the steel-suited gang. Ned escaped through the police lines but he came back to rescue his brother and friends. However, even his iron armour couldn't protect him. He eventually collapsed riddled with more than 28 bullets. Still alive, he was taken to Melbourne for medical treatment.

The only survivor of the siege, Ned was tried and sentenced to death despite the protests of thousands of loyal supporters. He was hanged, aged 25, on November 11, 1880, in Melbourne Jail.

But his legend lived on, bolstered by the books and films about his amazing life. The Glenrowan siege is re-enacted every decade and the area in which the gang roamed is still called Kelly Country.

GREAT IRISH HERO
WB YEATS

Poet, dramatist and Nobel Laureate, Dublin-born Yeats was a leader of the Irish Renaissance. He became one of the foremost writers of the 20th century.

THE INHABITANTS OF
GREAT BLASKET
ISLAND

A dormant but precious pearl in the misty span of Irish culture came alive in the summer of 2003.

People will return to Great Blasket Island, a bleak five-kilometre Celtic kingdom ruled for 50 years only by ghostly wailing winds.

This was the last outpost of true Irish life to be touched by the ravages of colonialism. Monks of the Celtic Church settled on the jagged slash of rock 1,000 years ago with little more than fish, seaweed, a few sheep and their prayers to hold body and soul together. For centuries tough folk there thrived by clinging to traditions and lore of which many today are ignorant. They helped each other with true Christian spirit.

A hundred years ago 176 people lived on Great Blasket, the most westerly point of Ireland. Around 80 per cent of

35

young people over the decades who left the island to seek wealth incredibly trod the same path. They went to Springfield, Massachusetts, where the distinct Blasket dialect became a common tongue. It can even be heard today.

By 1953, just 22 old folk remained and orders came from Dublin that a decent life for them could not be maintained, and they were shipped across to Dingle. But they and scores of generations before them are vividly remembered by Micheal de Mordha who runs the Blasket Centre on the mainland in Dun Chaoin, near Dingle. It celebrates the unique literary achievements of islanders and is dedicated to the native Irish language. Great Blasket folk and their descendents visited Dingle this summer. The actual anniversary of the last islanders to leave is in October 2003 but then rough weather roaring from the Atlantic will prevent a safe landing. There is no

The last of the islanders arrive in Dingle with their belongings.

A handful of the thirty tumbledown houses experts are
keen to restore.

safe jetty. Micheal said, 'We are hoping for the few
remaining islanders to pay a visit to the island in the
summer when the weather is good. We will give advice on
how to get there and we have experts on island life to give
lectures. The most amazing thing is the peace and
tranquillity you feel when you are standing on the island.
It is quite inspiring and you know why the pull of the
island is still so great to this day.'

Destructive seas and storms have reduced stone homes
in Great Blasket village to gaunt walls and rubble –
sanctuary only to abundant scampering rabbits. Micheal is
hoping to raise funds to restore the buildings for show as
they would have been in the early 1800s. His organisation
is in talks with the government over heritage finance.

Great Blasket, which at its widest point measures only

Blasket islanders working in teams founded a good trade in
lobsters with the French.

two kilometres, is one of a group of three islands. The
other two – known as Inishvickillane and Inishnabro – are
smaller and have never been inhabited.

The enchantment of Great Blasket is seen by many
through its surprising stock of writers, poets and
storytellers who kept old Irish culture alive in a pure
form.

Peig Sayers is one of the most famous writers and
storytellers. She told of the narrowness and hardship of
women's lives. Peig was born in Dunquin, Co. Kerry, in
1873 and married a man from Great Blasket in 1892. She
gave 50 years of her life to the island. She raised her
family there and suffered the deaths of five of them in a
peat-roofed hovel. Her husband died at a young age and
Peig coped alone. She stayed until 1942 and moved to
38

Vicarstown where she died in hospital with her son Micheal, a poet, at her side.

Peig was interested in storytelling as a performer and passing on old lore from her youth. Much of it was recorded and used by scholars. She left bleak Blasket gazing back across the Dingle peninsula to the island she believed would soon be forgotten. But the opposite has happened. A small shop, crumbling post office and homes still stand testimony to a lost era.

In the past the group of islands were referred to as Ferriter's Islands. From the end of the 13th century the Ferriter family leased the islands from the Earls of Desmond, and from Sir Richard Boyle after the dispossession of the last Desmond, Geraldine, at the end of the 16th century. They retained a castle there at Rinn

Children of Blasket Island who went to America.

The beautiful landscape disguises the harshness of life here.

an Chaisleain (Castle Point). But there are now no physical remains of that castle because the stones were carried off to build a Protestant soup kitchen in 1840.

The last of the Ferriters to control the Blaskets was the poet and rebel chieftain, Captain Piaras Feirtear. He was hanged at Cnocan na gCaorach in Killarney in 1653, after he and his followers were defeated at Ross Castle nearby by Crown forces.

The word Blasket itself is a mystery that has never been solved. The first sighting of the name appears on Italian maps in 1589 and it has been suggested, some historians believe, that it originated from the word 'brasker' meaning 'a dangerous place'.

Great Blasket has a covering of furze and heather with peat beneath much of it. The island has always been inundated with the rabbit but common animals on the mainland, like the rat and fox, have never been recorded

The writer Peig Sayers recorded stories of the tough life on
Great Blasket.

there. According to popular tradition the first people who lived on the Blasket islands herded animals, grew crops and hunted. In the beginning of the 19th century the first fishing vessels made their way to the island, starting a new seafaring tradition. Until then they had only fished from the rocks with hand lines

The number of people on the island has ebbed and flowed. There was a population of about 150 living there in 1840, but after the Great Famine that decreased to 100. Life for the islanders was always one of hardship and suffering but they had a love of life and richness of heritage. They survived mainly on fishing and small potato holdings. The mountain on the island was held in common by all islanders, allowing them the right to hunt for rabbits. Seaweed was used to fertilise the land because

it was such poor quality. There was an unwritten rule regarding the grazing of sheep: 25 sheep for each grazing cow and the man who did not have a cow was allowed to graze sheep only on the mountain. Donkeys were used to haul goods and provide transport.

For many years Dingle was the only market for their fish catches – until the French arrived with fish-storage ships in the 1920s. The islanders had an agreement to exchange goods and got nets, tobacco, wine, rum, or anything else they needed on credit. Debts were soon paid off with huge catches of prime lobsters.

But the big change came with the early 1930s. The island community began to decline and the young people were loath to marry. Only two couples married there between then and the time of its abandonment, with most making for America.

Entire households left in the 1940s and settled on the mainland. Their courage had deserted them a long time before the year of the great exodus in 1953.

The maximum number of houses on the island, at its peak, was 30. In 1909 the government's Congested Districts Board built five two-storey houses at the top of the village, looking down on the rest of the houses, but totally out of character with them. All the houses had a large kitchen with enough room to dance a set or accommodate animals at night or during bad weather. There was a loft above for sleeping and storing crops and fishing tackle.

Islanders had little experience of alcohol apart from the few drams they got from French fishermen. They only took a drink during rare days on the Dingle mainland, or at a wedding or wake.

The village was divided into lower and upper sections. There was always an edge to the competition between them and some locals always said that life was nobler in the lower village. Islanders formed their own town council which they called the Dail. All hotly debated issues were settled with handshakes.

During the summers island life was good with visitors from the mainland bringing plenty of goods and alcohol. Ceilidhs were common – but when huge leaden skies beckoned in winter and the last of the visitors had left, life closed in around them. It was a dreary time broken only by the skills of storytellers and their ales. The stories of Ireland that should never be forgotten.

GREAT IRISH HERO
CHARLES PARNELL

The young Protestant seen here would fight for Home Rule
through established political means and fiery speeches. He died due
to the hardships of the road whilst campaigning in Ireland.

JOHN BARRY

The poor Irishman who made waves as the father of US navy

An Irish lad born under the yoke of poverty and English cruelty grew up to dominate the Royal Navy. As the founding father of the American navy during the War of Independence, dauntless and daring Commodore John Barry captured, plundered and sank British warships. His seafarer's skills and tactics encouraged his commanders to defeat the British and send them packing. To this day a mighty statue of Barry stands guard in Philadelphia from where he sailed into history during the war from 1775–83.

He came into the world in 1745 at a tiny thatched cottage at Ballysampson on Our Lady's Island, Co. Wexford. He spent hours marvelling at the billowing ships voyaging from nearby Rosslare to trade across the world.

Commodore John Barry who captured, plundered and sank British warships.

And he yearned to join one – sailing to boy's own adventures in far-off climes.

His poor but peaceful life was shattered when his tenant-farmer father was evicted by the English landlord. The uprooted family moved to Rosslare to scrape a living

48

and by the age of 14 John Barry came to fully understand why the English oppressors were hated. His uncle, Nicholas Barry, was captain of a fishing skiff and young John seized his chance to get to sea as a cabin boy. He grew to 6ft 4in and rose to be first mate.

To the world he was a hard-working, friendly soul who earned respect. But in his heart ticked a time bomb of revenge to strike back at the enemy who put his family on the streets. At a young age he had been told of the massacre of 3,000 Wexfordians under an invading force led by Oliver Cromwell in 1649.

John left for America aged 21, seeking a new life in a country he would come to love and sacrifice everything for. He gained a commission as captain of the trading schooner *Barbados* in Philadelphia. John's easy manner enabled him to settle easily in the Philadelphia community. He sailed regularly to the West Indies, bringing back exotic goods. In 1772 John's abilities earned him the job as master of the prestige vessel the *Peig*.

In 1774 the first Continental Congress began, which was hoped would deal with the problems the colonies had with Britain.

Barry's last pre-revolutionary commission would be aboard the *Black Prince*, a fast 200-ton ship. He set a record by travelling 237 miles in 24 hours on a return trip from England. But John knew war was looming and he became friends with revolutionary leaders planning skirmishes.

He was devastated in 1775 when his first wife, Mary Cleary, who he had married in 1767, died at 29. Guilt over being at sea when she died stayed with him all his life. He later married again, socialite Sarah Keen Austin. Then his brother Patrick, a fellow sea captain, was lost at sea when his ship, the *Union*, sank as it sailed from Bordeaux, France.

John returned from a lengthy voyage to his home port to hear that the war of words had turned into full conflict. He was given the job of turning cargo ships into warships … and at last he had the chance of revenge and to rid America of British rule. He was commissioned as captain of the warship *Lexington* and he was itching to test out the vessel in battle. Guns blazing off the Cape of Virginia in April, 1776, he quelled and captured a British warship. He wrote at the time, 'This victory has had a tremendous psychological effect in boosting American morale, as it was the first capture of a British warship by a regularly commissioned American cruiser.' After that success he was given command of the huge 32-gun frigate *Effingham*.

But in 1777 he was forced to scuttle his new command in Philadelphia harbour when the British launched a surprise attack. George Washington now needed the famous captain to courier important messages through enemy-held waterways and seas.

In one escapade, John led men in rowing boats and longboats in the half-light of dawn. They overwhelmed the crews of three English ships. George Washington later sent him a letter stating that he was an incredible hero. 'May a suitable recompense always attend your bravery,' said Washington.

John, who put down three mutinies on his own during his career, had his most famous naval encounter off the

Miniature portrait of Barry as a young captain.

coast of Newfoundland in May, 1781. Barry's ship, the 36-gun frigate *Alliance*, took on two British ships, the sloops *Atlanta* and *Trespassy*. An *Alliance* broadside caused damage to both sloops, but then it was becalmed and the smaller ships were able to manoeuvre for the kill. John led

51

This was the kind of boat John Barry captained, ploughing into action against England off the coast of Newfoundland.

a desperate defence of the ship as cannon fire exploded all around. One explosion felled him with a shrapnel wound to his shoulder. He remained on deck for 20 minutes until he fell faint through loss of blood. The *Alliance*'s colours were shot away. John's second-in-command shouted to him, 'Sir, I have to report the ship is in frightful condition. Do I have permission to raise the flag of surrender?'

John mustered his strength to shout, 'No, sir, if this ship cannot be fought without me I will be brought on deck to do your duty.'

Suddenly, as if from a higher power, a gust of wind filled the *Alliance*'s sails, helping the ship to manoeuvre.

The battered *Alliance* swung round and fired salvo after salvo at the sloops. Four hours later they surrendered. One English captain offered John his sword as a sign of defeat but it was handed back with the words, 'I return it to you, sir. You have earned it, and your king ought to give you a better ship. Here is my cabin at your service. Use it as your own.'

John's final battle took place in 1783 as the *Alliance* was attacked by the English vessel *Sybil* while escorting a cargo ship. The battle lasted 45

A stature of John Barry in Philadelphia.

minutes before the *Sybil* pulled away to fight another day.

John returned to commercial shipping, helping to open trade routes to the Far East. But President George Washington had not forgotten the man many believed had played a major role in winning independence. In 1797, the President made him commodore of the navy and gave him his own vessel, the flagship christened the *United States*. The dreaming boy from Our Lady's Island had become one of the most powerful men in the world with hundreds of ships under his control.

In 1801 he returned from his last voyage and retired to a wave of goodwill wishes calling him the 'father of the navy'. He turned his attentions to helping foundations for the widows of seamen, raising money and help until he passed away in 1803. Chronic asthma claimed him. He was buried in St Mary's churchyard, Philadelphia, with full military honours. A grateful and powerful new nation said its thanks.

GREAT IRISH HERO
PHIL COULTER

The music supremo was born in Derry city. He has enjoyed
international success with hits like 'The Town I Loved So Well'.

DANIEL JOSEPH KEOGH

The St Patrick's Day
hero of Hill 355

He was just a country boy from Co. Longford who, like so many young Irishmen before him, set sail for America, eager for the great adventure of a new life.

Daniel Joseph Keogh took his adopted country to his heart. So when he was called up to fight in the Korean war, he viewed it as repaying his debt to the society which had welcomed him as one of its own. Such were his heroics on the notorious Hill 355 that he won the coveted Purple Heart bravery award and a street in Nevada was named after him.

He was killed in action on St Patrick's Day, 1953.

Daniel was born on September 13, 1928, the second child of Daniel J and Ellie Keogh of Cartron Upper, about a mile and a half outside the small village of Drumlish.

Hero of the Korean war: Danny Keogh.

DANIEL JOSEPH KEOGH

Danny's father earned his living farming a few isolated acres on the slopes of Cornhill. He was known as a kind, friendly boy. 'He was a really nice fellow. You just have to look at his photo to know what type of fellow he was,' said younger brother Michael, who still lives in the old homestead. Altogether the Keoghs had six sons and one daughter and all attended Doorok National School, which was nearby.

The name Danny had been in the Keogh family for six generations and he was named after his father to keep the tradition going. He grew up into a fine young man, over six feet tall, with a great passion for sport, and was popular with all who knew him.

He emigrated to America in April, 1949, aged just 20. Danny said his goodbyes to his family and embarked on the sea journey from Cobh Harbour to the bustling streets of New York. 'It was very hard to say goodbye to him and we were all very sad to see him go,' said Michael, now 72. From there he made his way west to the home of his maternal aunt, Mrs Anderson, who lived in a town called Sparks just outside Reno, Nevada. It had been a favoured destination for Irish emigrants, especially from Co. Longford, and many had found employment in the railyards of the Southern Pacific railway company.

Danny quickly adapted to his new life in Nevada and secured a job with the Sierra Power Company, and joined local sporting clubs. After a short time his aunt's husband – also from Drumlish – helped Danny get a job with the traditional employer of Longford men, the Southern Pacific railway.

After three years of working hard and enjoying his new life, Danny woke one morning to find his call-up papers for the US army on the doormat. The war in Korea between the US and North Korea's communist regime – backed by Chinese forces – had been raging for three years with no end in sight.

'Danny really enjoyed America and he felt that he owed something back to the country, so he had no qualms about going,' said Michael. He was sent to Fort Ord, about five miles from Monterey, California. There he had 16 weeks of basic training where he learned the art of war. He was given leave and went back to Sparks for a short stay in January, 1953.

Within one month Danny would be fighting in the hellhole of Korea. His unit stopped off in Japan where they received further training, and by early March Danny was preparing for his stint in the front lines at a camp near Seoul in Korea.

On the night of March 16 his company, which contained many raw recruits like Danny, were sent up the right-hand side of an American-held position, a hill called Kowangsan, known as Hill 355 or 'little Gibraltar'. It had been a Chinese stronghold taken by the 1st Commonwealth Division in fierce fighting in October, 1951. Since then the position had been held by various British, Commonwealth and American battalions, despite numerous attempts by the Chinese to retake it. As Danny and the rest of the infantry company came up the reverse slopes of the hill to relieve the company holding the position, a strong force of Chinese infantry launched a

The hero's brother: Michael Keogh at Danny's grave in Drumlish.

massive surprise attack, breaking through the American lines. A fierce close-quarters battle ensued and American and Chinese troops played a murderous game of hide and seek in the trenches and bunkers on the left side of Hill 355. The battle raged all night with both sides showering each other with grenades and mortars.

'According to his comrades, Danny fought bravely during the battle that ensued,' said Michael. 'He was always a man who would fight to the last.'

By dawn on St Patrick's Day, the Chinese attack had been driven off the hill with massive casualties to both forces. An estimated 500 Chinese and 300 Americans were killed. Among the casualties was Pte Danny Keogh, the farmer's son from Ireland, killed by shell fragments from enemy mortar fire.

Danny's body was moved to the American base camp by his comrades-in-arms who had seen him fight with unyielding courage. It was eventually flown back to the US.

'We were informed almost three weeks later and we were just devastated when we heard the news,' Michael said. 'We knew then there was only one way Danny was coming home to us and that was in a coffin.'

It was carried by train from Dublin to Co. Longford, accompanied by American soldiers who had fought with Danny in the conflict. The funeral cortege moved through the streets of Longford town and Danny made his final journey home to the Catholic church in Drumlish where he remained overnight, watched over by comrades from his unit. He was buried in a moving ceremony as volleys of rifle fire filled the air.

'The funeral was very upsetting but we knew he had done us proud, and his friends from his unit were great men,' said Michael.

At 10am on July 27, 1953, a month after Danny's body had been returned home, an armistice was signed. Danny was one of 33,629 American soldiers – 20 Irish-born – killed or missing in the Korean conflict. There is now a street named Keogh in Sparks, Nevada, after the man who laid down his life – like so many Irishmen had done in the past – for the American nation.

Every St Patrick's Day Michael visits his brother's grave in Drumlish. 'It has been a long time but I still miss him. He was so loved and this year being the 50th anniversary of his death will be very hard for me,' said Michael.

As well as the Purple Heart, Danny was posthumously awarded the Gold Star for his bravery. He had spent a cold night on the hill fighting the constant barrage of attacks from the die-hard Chinese attackers. Men where beginning to fall around him as the Chinese pushed on with their bloody attack.

A chaplain in Danny's unit wrote to his family expressing his deep regret for the loss. 'The memory of your son's heroic death will always be a source of inspiration to this regiment,' he wrote. 'He died bravely in defence of the principles we hold dear, and which will ultimately triumph in a peaceful world.'

GREAT IRISH HERO
RORY GALLAGHER

The shy Cork-born blues and rock singer helped put Ireland on the map with his legendary band Taste. He died after complications during a liver transplant.

WILLIAM BROWN

The Irish cabin boy who
sank the Spanish fleet

An Irish lad born into hardship rose to become one of the most revered men in the Americas.

Courageous seafarer William Brown founded the Argentine navy and became an admiral.

In Argentina, he is honoured to this day as someone who played a huge part in the country's struggle to gain its freedom from colonial Spain. Such prominence was an astonishing feat for the boy from the small town of Foxford on the banks of the salmon-rich River Moy in Co. Mayo.

To commemorate Brown, a memorial bronze bust stands in the town, cared for by the Foxford Admiral Brown Society, and a museum is planned. And in Argentina's capital Buenos Aires, a huge statue of the Irish hero is the focus of annual ceremonies in his honour.

Brown was born on June 22, 1777, and later spoke of remembering the cruelty in his home country from an early age. The late 18th century in the west of Ireland was a period of deprivation and poverty for Catholics because of the infamous penal laws. So, when Brown was nine his father took the family to America and they settled in Philadelphia. They were invited by an old friend from Ireland who became their benefactor, providing them with food and accommodation. But within two years the friend contracted yellow fever and died, leaving the Browns struggling in their adopted land.

Worse was to come. William's father also succumbed to the disease and the desperate family lost their main breadwinner.

When a ship's captain offered the youngster work as a cabin boy he jumped at the chance to help support his mother. It was the start of a career that would bring the young Brown much danger alongside great rewards. Over the next few years his intelligence and dedication to duty saw him rise to become captain of a merchant vessel.

During the Napoleonic wars in Europe both Brown and his ship were seized by a French man o' war. He was captured and taken to Metzjail. Incredibly, he managed to escape from his cell, disguised in the uniform of a French officer but he was dramatically recaptured and sent to the Verdun prison fortress. While being held captive there he met an English colonel named Clutchwell and together they planned another daredevil escape.

They fled under the noses of the French and spent months trying to reach the relative safety of Germany.

The cottage in which Brown was born.

From Germany, Brown made his way to South America, where he felt he could make a small fortune as a seafarer transporting goods. He became part-owner of a ship called the *Eliza* and began trading between Montevideo and Buenos Aires.

When the *Eliza* met with disaster and went aground, Brown carried his precious cargo of merchandise inland and sold it for profit. He next crossed the Andes mountains and went into Chile. By now he had accumulated sufficient capital to enable him to purchase a schooner called the *Industria* with which he opened a regular sailing-packet service between Uruguay and Argentina – the first venture of its kind in South America.

But then the Spanish stepped in, sensing a threat to their merchant shipping interests. Spanish troops landed on the coast of Argentina and destroyed Brown's schooner, and took drastic effects to stifle Argentina's attempts to defend

67

her coasts against Spanish raiders. As a result of this attack, Argentina resolved to provide ships to protect her coasts and trade, with Brown being appointed the first navy commander. The Irishman immediately tried to negotiate with Spanish navy commander Jacinto Romarate, but to no avail. Then he attacked the formidable Spanish fleet with his ill-equipped navy and patchwork crews.

On March 8,1813, Brown bravely set sail with his small fleet of part-time sailors, aiming to strike a blow against the mighty Spanish fleet. Within 48 hours he was engaged in an awesome battle. Spanish land and sea forces lay in wait at Martin Garcia, a fortified island 25 miles from Buenos Aires and known as the Gibraltar of the River Plate.

Brown's flagship, the *Hercules*, was badly battered and ran aground. He and his men attacked vigorously by land and sea on March 14, and after a stiff contest succeeded in gaining possession of Martin Garcia.

Buenos Aires in the 1830s: a thriving port.

Admiral Brown.

The Spanish captain Jacinto Romarate, who was defeated by Brown.

Then Romarate hastened with his ships to Montevideo, hotly pursued by Brown and his fleet. Brown blockaded Montevideo, threatening it with starvation. Then, pretending he was retreating, he drew the Spaniards into a trap away from the protection of the fort guns.

On May 16, a fierce engagement took place, during which a cannon ball shattered Brown's left leg. Despite the agony of the terrible injury he never left his post and carried on giving orders. In a fearful panic, the Spanish squadron rushed for a safe haven in port, but three of their ships were captured. As a direct result of this engagement the River Plate was freed from Spanish domination and the Argentinean fleet rode the waves victorious.

Montevideo had also fallen and Brown was hailed as the

'Hercules' the flagship of Brown's poorly funded fleet – it still managed to defeat the mighty Spanish fleet.

hero of Argentina. Honours were showered on him. He was promoted to the rank of colonel and confirmed in his post as naval commander. His flagship *Hercules* was presented to him as a personal gift for his brave and gallant services against the traditional oppressor and enemy, Spain.

Brown was not destined to remain inactive for long. Uruguay had been a bone of contention between Spain and Portugal for three centuries. Now Brazil and Argentine squared up for control of the country.

On December 11, 1825, war broke out between the two. The Brazilians initiated operations by blockading Argentine ports. In this dire emergency, Argentina – under the guidance and inspiration of Brown – improvised a new fleet of which he took supreme command as admiral.

As a counter-move to the blockade, he attacked the Brazilian coast, shattered Brazilian shipping and, at the hard-fought Battle of Juncal, captured the entire opposing Brazilian fleet and took the commander prisoner. By June, 1826, the two sides agreed a fragile peace.

To grapple with the difficult situation that had arisen, Brown was asked to become Governor of Buenos Aires, the only foreigner ever entrusted with this high office. But finding the problems that surrounded him too complex to deal with, he soon resigned and withdrew to his country residence to enjoy some tranquillity. He left the opposing factions to finish the dog-fight.

In 1847 he made an emotional return to his home of Foxford, where he tried to help his homeland through some of its darkest days. Having returned to his adopted

72

country, he died there ten years later, in 1857, and was buried in the country's premier cemetery at Recvoleta, which is reserved for the great and the good.

Admiral Brown was a tall, well-built, beetle-browed man with burning dark eyes. He had a nervous and restless manner that made every movement seem urgent. His memory is as strong as ever for South Americans. When an Argentine navy ship, the *Libertad*, with a crew of 300, dropped anchor in Ireland's Kilala Bay on a courtesy visit in 1998, they paid tribute to Admiral Brown. At a ceremony of remembrance Javier Armando Valladares, the *Libertad*'s second-in-command, said, 'He came to Argentina to find a safe place to live but found himself fighting to help our country win its freedom.'

Today in Argentina there are around 400,000 people of Irish descent, and Irish surnames are common, with St Patrick's Day widely celebrated. Back in Foxford the compliment is returned. When Argentina play a big soccer match the town is decorated with the country's blue and white colours.

GREAT IRISH HERO
ERSKINE CHILDERS

The politician and author who helped to win Irish Independence and fought on the side of de Valera in the Irish civil war. He was executed by Free State forces.

TOM BARRY

The rebel who defied the
might of an empire

Staunch Irish country boy Tom Barry achieved what countless armies failed to do. He struck dread into the heart of the British Empire. The English, he said, would only heed force and the smoking barrel of a gun. So Tom out-thought and out-fought marauding Crown Forces units in the wooded hills of West Cork and along the road to Limerick. And he used hit-and-run and ambush tactics the British army had taught him during three years' fighting in Iraq, during the First World War.

Tom was barely 22 when he commanded 30 young men of steel in the War of Independence and Partition in 1919. They were so effective in battle that they helped ebb the tide of war in favour of Irish patriots. Forces sent to Ireland weren't much more than wanton

Tom Barry leading veterans of the Kilmichael ambush to the unveiling of the memorial at Crossbarry in July 1966.

killers and criminals with little discipline. But they learned caution when taking on the West Cork flying column, headed by Barry.

Tom Barry was born in 1897 in the quiet coastal town of Rosscarbery, which grew from a 6th-century monastery and picturesque square. Little is known of his family and childhood as he rarely spoke of them, but he was one of 14 children and his father was a Royal Irish Constabulary officer in the pay of the British. He did not speak of him but mused on a love of the rugged Cork coastline.

In 1915 Tom joined the British army and said later, 'I cannot pretend I joined it for any noble reason but just the simple fact that I wanted to see what war was like.' He was demobbed in 1918 and was consumed by the struggle for freedom.

Tom joined the IRA and made up his mind to fight the army with which he had only recently marched. Rebel groups the length and breadth of Ireland went into action as Ireland began the most turbulent period in its history.

On January 21, 1919, the IRA shot dead two Irish policemen in Co. Tipperary and that marked the beginning of the War of Independence. The Catholic Church condemned the IRA. Locals who knew the perpetrators were appalled. But they kept quiet. The British clamped down and the guerrilla war in Cork and Tipperary flared.

With the post-war British army in a shambles, the country's Prime Minster David Lloyd George sent over the auxiliaries – 1,500 ex-First World War soldiers – in groups to terrorise the Irish into submission in the most troublesome spots. But the men of Cork, like Michael Collins, Tom Barry and many others did not bow. The

British soldiers search for arms in cabbages in 1919.

British army groups in black police and tan army uniforms became known as the Black and Tans, whose vicious behaviour labelled them as little more than gangsters.

Tom Barry drew around him 30 young men to fight back. The band roamed the hills of West Cork, not able to return home for fear of endangering loved ones. It was a life of hardship and rough living. Tom stayed only a few hours in each place.

The Black and Tans were told that the Irish rebels were a small force who would not pose much of a challenge. They quickly set about imposing their brutal rule with deeds that beggared belief. They shot farm labourers for fun as they passed in vehicles without fear of justice taking a hand. They burned the city of Cork down, claiming it was in retaliation for the murder of some of their troops. In Ballycannion they captured six IRA men and took

Cork city burnt to the ground by the British in 1920.

turns to torture them before they were executed. Many Black and Tans got rich by robbing banks and post offices with impunity and sending the proceeds to England. They claimed it was a war tax.

Tom Barry knew fear could cripple the war effort and justice was needed to bring down these soldiers. He was a master of strategy who could have his volunteers ready at a moment's notice.

On a cold evening in November, 1920, 18 auxiliaries went on patrol in two trucks. They had no knowledge of the West Cork flying column being in the area and lying in wait. Tom Barry's men were armed only with old Lee-Enfield .303 rifles, and 29 of the 30 had not yet fired a shot in anger. They waited on a bend in the Kilmichael road near the village of Macroom, hiding in bushes and in surrounding hills. Tom followed exactly the tactics he had witnessed in Iraq.

As the Black and Tans auxiliaries' trucks came round the comer, the volunteers opened fire. The auxiliaries jumped from their vehicles expecting the IRA to flee from their superior armed force. But there was no retreat. The hidden foe kept up accurate fire. Five Black and Tans died in a couple of minutes.

At one stage the auxiliaries, who were pinned down behind their trucks, shouted that they were surrendering. When some volunteers stood up to accept the surrender the auxiliaries opened fire, killing three of them and wounding another. No further mercy was shown. The auxiliaries were wiped out.

The British Cabinet was recalled as news filtered

through that one of their units had been massacred by a bunch of part-time soldiers from Cork. It was seeking a truce with Dail Eireann.

Tom Barry was helping bring the enemy of Ireland to its knees. He and his men became some of the most wanted in Ireland, joining a list that included Collins and de Valera. They launched attacks on outposts of Royal Irish Constabulary units and took arms and ammunition.

A truce was called in December, 1921. For six months peace negotiations were hammered out with Tom's friend Michael Collins. Collins returned from London with a deal that fell short of what Tom believed he had been fighting for. He could not believe that he had risked his life and those of his men for what he saw as settling for just dominion status and not a Republic.

Ireland descended into a bloody civil war as brother fought brother. Although it pained Tom he decided to take up arms against the newly-formed Free State and his former comrades, including Collins, who was ambushed at Beal na mBlath in Co. Cork. Tom Barry and 300 other IRA men were locked up at the Curragh soon after the civil war began. In May, 1922, the civil war ended and a year later Tom was set free and given the rank of general.

He married Leslie De Barra, the widow of an IRA man. He was appointed as superintendent with Cork harbour commissioners and held the post until 1965. He had maintained his active membership in the IRA until 1938 when he resigned because he disagreed with a bombing campaign in England. He said he did not want innocent people to be killed in the name of Irish freedom. His

Tom Barry as he was when he led the West Cork flying column of
volunteers on raids.

thoughts were published in Guerrilla Days in Ireland, which he wrote in 1949. He explained in detail his roles in the War of Independence and the ensuing civil war. Tom Barry lived out the rest of his days quietly and died in Cork Hospital on July 20, 1980, survived by his wife.

The rebel was finally at peace.

JOHN BOYLE O'REILLY

A long voyage to freedom

Romance and soft words filled the sweet verse of Irish poet and dreamer John Boyle O'Reilly. But when his thoughts turned to the great Fenian cause he became a formidable man of steel and action. He plotted a bold and brave mission to sail halfway round the world to Australia to pluck six Irish heroes, victims of the evil transportation policy, from a dank British prison. They broke free from a chain gang and were ferried to a ship by sympathisers to blow on the winds to freedom. He outwitted the British navy with high seas' daring and became an all-time Irish-American champion of the free.

A statue in Boston commemorates the life of O'Reilly that was beyond the scope of fiction. He was a visionary who lived the language of his own axiom: A dreamer lives for ever. And a toiler dies in a day.

GREAT IRISH HEROES

John Boyle O'Reilly was born the son of a schoolmaster at Douth Castle, Co. Meath, on June 24, 1844. He was bright, learned easily and as a lad became a printer on the Drogheda Argus. Even then he had begun to turn his fiery pen to bolstering the Fenian doctrine which was born among Irish migrants in New York. It spread across the world wherever Irish folk settled.

After a spell on the *Guardian* paper in Lancashire, O'Reilly became a trooper in the Prince of Wales 11th Hussars – placed there as a spy by the Fenian Society. He tried to draw fellow Irish troopers to the cause then found himself betrayed as a secret freedom fighter. He was court-martialled and sentenced to death. With only hours to the sentence being carried out it was commuted to 20 years' penal servitude in Australia as an act of 'mercy'. He was just 22.

The flag that O'Reilly raised on his ship the Catalpa which made the British turn away.

John Boyle O'Reilly.

The rescue ship Catalpa leaving New Bedford under full sail.

O'Reilly, with injustice and hatred now burned into his soul, arrived at the notorious Freemantle jail with 63 fellow Fenians rounded up by the British. They would be the last convicts transported to the colonies. The prisoners spent their days in blistering heat breaking rocks and building roads.

By early 1869, O'Reilly had had enough of the fruitless labour designed to break the prisoners' spirits. Having been moved near the port of Bunbury, he was able to form an escape plan after getting word from friendly local Irish folk that a ship from America would be setting sail in days. With cash from locals for bribes he fled. The ship's captain stowed him on board for a fee and they set sail for Boston.

O'Reilly made a new life for himself in the vibrant city of New York where he became a much respected editor of the *Pilot* newspaper.

But his passion for Ireland and his fellow Fenian

warriors would never leave his heart. In late 1869, the British government granted conditional pardons to any Fenian who had not been found guilty of planting explosives or carrying out shootings. This meant hundreds were freed under the amnesty. But six Fenian volunteers were left to rot. They were Thomas Darragh, Martin Hogan, Michael Harrington, Thomas Hasset, Robert Cranston and James Wilson. O'Reilly knew of their torment and loneliness and formed a plan bordering on the suicidal in its audacity to snatch them from British gaolers. Fenian Society leaders told him to hold fire and

Monument in New Bedford to the seven rescued.

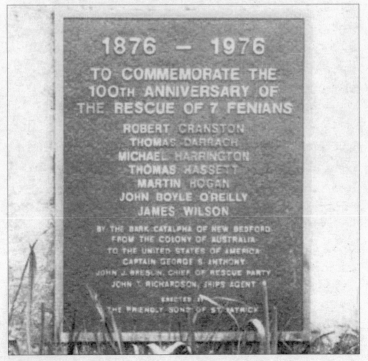

Capt. George Anthony and his New Bedford Whaler the Catalpa

The Friendly Sons
of Saint Patrick

Captain George Anthony.

Rescued: Thomas Hasset, Thomas Darragh and Michael Harrington.

Far left, James Wilson, second from right, Martin Hogan and second from left, Robert Cranston.

said they believed the British would release the six anyway because of the amnesty. They didn't.

Four years later the society gave O'Reilly's master plan the all clear and full backing. With cash from a legion of Irish-Americans, O'Reilly bought for €5,250 the *Catalpa*, the very sailing ship that had brought him to freedom. He spent another €15,000 disguising it as a whaling ship with harpoons and gear to fool British informers. On the dawn high tide of April 29, 1875, the *Catalpa* slipped out of harbour at New Bedford, Massachusetts, bound for a glorious passage in Irish history.

Captain George S Anthony, a trusted Fenian sympathiser, told the crew only that they were heading for the southern oceans and the rich pickings of pods of whales. With plenty of food and grog and fair weather, they showed little concern for their voyage or destination.

Three months later the *Catalpa* neared Australia and berthed at the little-used deep-water harbour at Bunbury, a community along the coast from busy Freemantle. A message was despatched to Freemantle by Fenian agents in Bunbury who had already been sent there from New York. A massive Irish network given detailed orders by O'Reilly was told, 'The prison break is ON.' They managed to get word to the prisoners inside, who had been anxiously waiting for good news.

O'Reilly's plan was a stroke of genius, with dozens of men seemingly appearing from nowhere to assist with the grand scheme. Captain Anthony sailed for Freemantle

A Victorian depiction of the getaway, the six prisoners narrowly avoid British militiamen.

where he waited nervously for the escapees. The plan was for agents lying in wait to help the six overpower a chain-gang guard and flee. The authorities believed little supervision was needed because the men would not escape as there was nowhere to go in the harsh climate. But they did not count on the ingenuity of their former prisoner, O'Reilly. With split-second timing, the men overpowered the guard and Fenian supporters arrived with guns and carriages. Dusty roads took them to a remote point on Freemantle Bay where men were waiting to row them to the *Caltalpa*. The alarm was raised at the prison and the British sent an armed steamship, the *Georgette*, to intercept the sailing ship wallowing with little wind for a clear getaway. A steam-powered police cutter also joined in the chase.

Within hours a storm blew up making good progress impossible under sail. Captain Anthony had a stroke of luck when the *Georgette* had to return to port to refuel. But by the following day it had caught up again – just 18 miles from Freemantle. The *Caltalpa* zigzagged to avoid capture. All seemed lost as the cutter and the *Georgette* closed in, firing shots across the *Caltalpa*'s bows. Then Captain Anthony pulled off the master stroke impressed on him by O'Reilly if the mission seemed in jeopardy.

A 10ft stars and stripes flag was unfurled, signalling to the British that he was in international waters and that this would be seen as an attack on America. Incredibly, as O'Reilly predicted, the British turned away.

As their smoke drifted away on the horizon Captain Anthony's crew, now fully aware of the mission, cheered.

There was a great celebration on board. The most daring and intricate plan in the history of the Irish bid for freedom was a success. Winds rose from the south and the *Caltalpa* sliced her way home under full sail.

A jubilant crowd of tens of thousands flocked to New Bedford to see the heroes land. One of the first to greet them was O'Reilly, now a married man with four young daughters. He greeted each of the six with a hug of congratulations.

Fenian Society fellows marvelled at his steely toughness in the homeland cause. He was a hard man. Yet the extraordinary O'Reilly had written this gentle verse to his wife Mary:

The red rose whispers of passion, And the white rose breathes of love.

Oh, the red rose is a falcon, And the white rose is a dove.

But I send you a cream-white rosebud With a flush on its petal tips.

For the love that is purest and sweetest Has a kiss of desire on the lips.

John Boyle O'Reilly, dreamer, died in New York in 1886, aged just 42. But his legend will live for ever.

THOMAS SWEENY

**Yankee general who went into battle
for Irish homeland**

Wild one-armed Thomas Sweeny was a one-man
war machine. He fought and won 100 battles,
leading from the front with blood-curdling battle cries
roared in Gaelic.

The true valour of the bold lad from Cork took him
through the ranks to be a brigadier-general with the
American Civil War Yankee army. But when the slaughter
ended in 1865 and brother stopped killing brother,
action-man Sweeny, 45, just could not stop fighting. He
turned his military mettle on the enemy etched into his
soul – the hated English who destroyed his homeland.

Sweeny raised a Fenian army of thousands of new-world
Irishmen fresh from the civil war to drive the occupying
British army from Canada.

A mighty act of planned revenge in 1866 sent them

swarming across the border into lower Ontario with the aim of booting out the British. But British spies had wind of the raiders and columns of reinforcements were sent in to counter the threat. Sweeny's forces did not lack zeal but were overwhelmed by the firepower and numbers of the British. He was livid. His final battle tactics had failed. An audacious strategy to remove the last British foothold from the North American map was over and Sweeny was driven back. He was arrested by American forces who wanted no truck with the British army and ordered him to stop fighting.

Sweeny was later released and his rank was restored by presidential decree. He retired in the summer of 1870 to his home in Long Island, New York, where he was surrounded by Irish migrants with fresh tales and songs from the old country.

Thomas William Sweeny died in April, 1892, and was buried with full military honours. He was 72. With all the pomp, America showed its gratitude to a courageous and devoted immigrant son.

Sweeny's was an astonishing life that like so many began in poverty and daily hunger in rural Ireland. He was born in 1820. As a fascinated small boy he heard from others about the United States – the land of the free, he was told, with food and jobs for all at every turn for anyone willing just to make the sea journey.

By the time he was 12 his family had had enough of their meagre life in Ireland and took a ship from Cork. It was a rough crossing for the Sweenys. They lived in squalid conditions in New York where young Thomas was

Sweeny's 52nd Illinois Volunteers capture Fort Donelson. Hundreds died and he took 6,000 prisoners.

wary enough to steer clear of gangs and was determined to make a name for himself. He worked diligently as an apprentice printer for several years but yearned for excitement.

Young Sweeny saw a poster asking for recruits to join the American army. So at 18 he joined up. He was despatched to the front lines of the war between the US and Mexico in 1846 and quickly proved his bravery in battle. He enjoyed giving orders and found that other enlisted men would follow him. As the battles raged Sweeny was promoted to second-lieutenant with A Company, First New York Volunteers.

He was in the epic siege of Vera Cruz and the storming of Churubusco, where he was wounded by a musket ball that shattered his right arm. It was a devastating blow to the young officer when sawbones (army medics) amputated above the elbow. But the disability did not hold Sweeny back. He recovered to rejoin his unit and earned the nickname Fighting Tom. He returned to New York as a hero and was given a grand reception by the printers of the city and a silver medal from the governor of New York, and promoted to captain.

After the Mexican battles Sweeny was sent on a new mission to fight Indians attacking settlers of the western plains. During the 1850s his valour and undoubted bravery won him many admirers among his own ranks and further up the chain of command.

Indians besieged his camp for six months, but he miraculously survived the ordeal and was rescued when government troops broke through to rescue him and his men.

In 1857 Sweeny witnessed history being made as the Great Treaty with the Sioux Nations was signed in his presence, promising the defeated Indians land for their people in exchange for peace. It was during the Indian

The one-armed fighter's troops under Sweeny tasted success after success.

Brigadier General Thomas W. Sweeny!

wars that Sweeny first yelled his orders in Gaelic and taught his officers what they meant.

Peace had finally come to Sweeny's adopted land but it would not last long. In 1861 the North and the South were at war. Sweeny was ordered to St Louis and given command of a munitions dump, which had enough arms and ammunition to arm 60,000 men. And with just over 40 conscripted troops he managed to keep the guns from falling into enemy hands. They successfully forced off 3,000 militia men waiting to advance on the arms dump. What Sweeny lacked in men he made up for in gunpowder, warning the militia that if they attempted to seize the arms he would blow everyone to kingdom come. It worked. Knowing his wild reputation, his enemies did not dare approach.

In May, 1861, he was made a brigadier-general and accepted the command- of the 52nd Illinois Volunteers, attached to the army of General Grant. Sweeny captured Fort Donelson and took 6,000 prisoners.

Success after success followed the charismatic man. He was wounded on a number of occasions, including one day when he was shot several times before collapsing.

His men presented him with a Tiffany sword, field glass and a sash as an expression of their regard for him as an officer and a gentleman. A note read, 'If the severity of your discipline was at first unpleasant, experience has convinced us both of its importance and necessity; thereby serving to increase our respect for you as an honest, faithful and impartial commander.'

In a letter dated September 18, 1863, Sweeny wrote a

touching letter of thanks to the officers of the 52nd Illinois. He wrote, 'I shall ever prize and guard them as the very apple of mine eye for they speak to me through many of the best and sweetest associations of my life.'

In 1864 his division drove back the enemy at the city of Atlanta with a ferocious slaughter, capturing four of the Confederates' flags and 900 prisoners. But this would turn out to be the Corkman's last battle in the civil war. Everyone expected him to hang up his sword in 1865. But they had not reckoned on his inner battle with the English. He went to his grave without settling that score. But his memory lives on in Springfield, Missouri, at General Sweeny's Museum.

GREAT IRISH HERO
NEIL JORDAN

Writer and director Neil Jordan's hits include *The Crying Game* and *Michael Collins*. He has paved the way for new Irish talent and currently lives in Dublin.

ELIZA ALICIA LYNCH

From vice to Evita

A skinny, flame-haired waif from the Great Hunger blossomed into the self-styled Empress of South America.

Neighbouring farm folk had wondered if half-starved, bandy-legged Co. Cork colleen Eliza Alicia Lynch would survive. They said the child in rags was so thin she couldn't stop a pig in a passage. But 15 years later the feisty Irish beauty was ensconced in a servant-laden palace and flouncing in luxurious silks. She ordered fine food by the shipload and hoarded gold and jewels by the chest. She also grabbed vast tracts of land. And she even helped rouse the barefoot peasants of Paraguay and their tetchy cigar-smoking women to go to war. For Eliza Lynch held sway over a country six times the size of the Irish Republic. She had become the world's first material girl ... an early

The young Eliza Lynch who became one of the wealthiest women in the world during her lifetime as the consort of the Paraguay president Francisco Solano Lopez.

version of Argentina's Evita. How on earth did she do it?

It is an astonishing story of a simple Irish girl with the iron will to be rid of the English and the shackles of poverty – at any cost.

She was born in 1835 into a large family with nothing but a few acres of land to eke out an existence. By the age of 19 she had survived the cruel squalor of the famine and headed by ship for Paris. Some say she worked her passage as a vice girl.

In France she quickly met and captivated a young army officer. They wed and Eliza became the French lieutenant's woman. Within months she had ditched him and his meagre income for a mysterious, beguiling Russian who fed her a pack of lies about riches and royal connections.

Eliza's flightiness cost her dearly. The Russian vanished – and she did not even know his real name. Penury forced her to take to the streets and she knew she had to quickly find a man with money or sink into the morass and disease of Paris street life. Eliza's tough upbringing gave her the will to grab the main chance.

It came when a dour and swarthy man called Francisco Lopez paid her much attention. Eliza showed little enthusiasm for him apart from lightening his purse for her large fees. He turned out to be a real diamond, though. Another street girl told her Francisco was the son of the dictator of Paraguay and suddenly, in Eliza's eyes, he turned into a handsome suitor and her path to enormous wealth.

In 1854 the couple set sail for Paraguay. Eliza took a grand piano to add a touch of class for the locals to admire in the capital, Asuncion. But they were not impressed and shunned all Eliza's offers to dine with her. And Francisco's mother and sisters despised her. They called her the Irish whore but never to her face.

When Francisco's father died, he took over the country. Her lust for wealth satisfied, Eliza craved power and influence and took on the title of the Empress of South America.

One day Eliza organised a splendid banquet on board a ship. But when the guests all turned their noses up at her feast she order all the food and drink to be cast overboard.

The dictator Francisco Lopez who adored and worshipped Eliza.

Eliza Lynch as a middle-aged woman.

Then, in true Eliza fashion, she told the captain to anchor the boat away from the harbour so the blistering midday heat scorched the guests.

Eliza began to mirror her husband's cruelty but her greed far exceeded his. She encouraged him to grab land from neighbours and in 1865 he launched an attack on giant neighbour Brazil. It was a crazy move. Brazil's national guard numbered 450,000 – the same figure as Paraguay's entire population.

Eliza launched herself into the campaign, telling the women of Paraguay that they must hand over their jewellery for the war effort. But she kept the jewels for herself. She then seized the lands of Spanish aristocrats and sent them to the frontline and certain death – in bare feet. Her lands totalled 80million acres, all stolen.

Eva Peron in Argentina 100 years later – in some ways a parallel life to Eliza's.

Argentina and Uruguay joined in the War of the Triple Alliance and Paraguay was doomed. Women and children pressed into fighting were slaughtered as Eliza sat on wealth that made her the richest woman in the world by far, while three quarters of her people perished.

As the war drew to a bloody end in 1869, the megalomaniac duo began to fear people closest to them. They executed some of their aides and even slaughtered Francisco's relatives. However, Eliza's riches were seized by the victorious armies so, with a small band of warriors, the couple fled into the mountains.

In 1870, the end finally came for Francisco Lopez. He was captured and hanged. But Eliza managed to flee back to Paris – with just the clothes she stood in.

Incredibly, Eliza returned several years later to the country she had pillaged and demanded her wealth back. But orphans and widows demanded that she should be sacrificed. So brazen Eliza again fled back to Paris to the position she was in 20 years earlier. She fell away into obscurity and abject poverty, her charms gone, and in 1885 she died.

But the astonishing tale of little Eliza Alicia Lynch from Cork was not buried and forgotten. In 1961, the Paraguayan authorities had her remains taken from Paris to Asuncion for a State burial in a grand mausoleum. Her epitaph says she had been a true heroine, selfless companion of 'the greatest hero of the nation'. Time had healed wounds and muddied the truths of the past. A rich joke by Eliza from beyond the grave.

GREAT IRISH HERO
LIAM BRADY

One of Ireland's greatest footballers, the Dubliner enjoyed memorable
moments with Arsenal and Italians Juventus. He made 72
appearances for his country before retiring.

THE ROYAL DUBLIN
FUSILIERS

Ireland's forgotten dead

Teenage Irish soldiers fell like crumpled autumn leaves. The hot Helles Beach sand on the Gallipoli Peninsula turned red with their blood. The venom of Turkish machine guns spitting death halved the 1,012 strength of the 1st Battalion, Royal Dublin Fusiliers, in 15 minutes. Hellish shell-fire accounted for the Dubs missed by bullets.

A survivor wrote home to his mother, 'We were slaughtered like trapped rats.'

It was their first taste of war, clutching shiny Lee-Enfield .303 rifles they had not yet fired in anger. Within weeks only 11 were left to return to the green of home, to find the Dubs were already being forgotten.

That cruel day – April 15, 1915 – in Ireland's long and often sorrowful history is rarely remembered. Because

Hundreds of young men walked straight into death from the doors of the beached River Clyde.

of political history, the country has chosen to make its lost army of the Great War the neglected dead. But the Royal Dublin Fusiliers Association have called for a museum to be set up as a permanent memorial to the sacrifice of the Dubs. A spokesman said, 'We badly need a museum for all our memorabilia, so we can show the Irish public what these men fought and died for. There is not one monument for the men who fell while wearing the Fusiliers uniform. We believe times are changing and people realise these men went off to die for Ireland believing that this would free the country from British rule.'

But when they returned to their native streets of Dublin it was evident that the same people who had earlier cheered them on now despised them. 'It was a very difficult time for these soldiers, it must have been like US soldiers returning after Vietnam,' the spokesman said. A total of 11 battalions of the Royal Dublin Fusiliers were formed to fight in the First World War. At least 4,780 of the men died. They were awarded 49 battle honours and three Victoria Crosses, the highest bravery award. Up to 200,000 Irishmen altogether fought with the Allies and 35,500 were killed over the four years.

Young men filled with the fervour of youth rushed to join the Dublin Fusiliers as news of the war spread. Home Rule party leaders believed it would be over by Christmas of 1914, so they urged young men to volunteer to aid the cause of a free Ireland by joining the Allies.

A historian said, 'Many hoped to achieve Irish freedom

A soldier's farewell to a fallen friend

by helping Britain in her hour of need. Others joined just for the adventure or to escape unemployment queues. Little did they know the true horrors they would witness, images that would haunt for the rest of their lives the lucky few who managed to make it back to their native land.'

Thousands of young men had flocked to join the Dublin Fusiliers and were sent to Cork for basic training. The camaraderie was great. To many it was just a lark. Senior commanders of the British forces ordered that there should be no send-off parades at home for Irish regiments because they feared Ireland was riddled with German spies. But the people of Dublin were having none of that. In true Irish fashion they gave the men of the brave Fusiliers a send-off they would never forget. One newspaper of the time reported, 'Led by the band of the 12th Lancers and the Pipers of the Trinity College Training Corps, they marched off from the Royal Barracks. Along the quays, crowds on the pavements and spectators in the windows cheered and waved. Little boys strutted along marching with the column.' But for many who lined the streets of Dublin that day it would be the last time they saw their loved ones.

After further training in Hampshire, England, the 1st and 2nd battalions set sail for the unknown on July 10. The confident young men were expecting an easy victory as their leaders had led them to believe. The Allies considered that an attack on Turkey would force the Germans to divert troops from the Western front to help their allies Turkey stave off the British forces. This would in turn allow the British to make a breakthrough in

Winston Churchill planned the debacle.

German lines in Europe, thus ending the murderous war.

Within weeks the Irish lads were on the beaches at Gallipoli in the disastrous assault planned by Britain's then naval chief Winston Churchill, who failed to heed warnings of the strength and will of Turkish forces.

As the Dubliners steamed nearer to the shoreline of Gallipoli Peninsula they sat in awe and fear as flashes of artillery fire and explosions thundered all around. The sight of hundreds of injured men and the stench of war and death began to filter towards them on the decks of

1st Battalion, Royal Dublin Fusiliers, marched off to war from their city barracks in 1915. Less than a dozen returned.

their ships as they waited to disembark. Hundreds of men poured from special doors built into the beached troop ship *River Clyde*. Their first steps on dry land were met with a hail of bullets. They tried desperately to reach the safety of the sand dunes at the head of the beach, but many were struck down by a barrage of deadly fire from an unseen, well-fortified enemy.

'What no one had told the young Irishmen was that the Turkish army were willing to fight to the very death to defend their homeland,' said the history expert. Fortified positions that should have been destroyed by a promised massive naval bombardment were untouched. Artillery pieces to support the landings went to France instead on the wrong ships. The men had no maps of the Gallipoli Peninsula or up-to-date intelligence on where to land and attack. And they did not even have orders about what to do and where to head when they did land.

To further imperil the Fusiliers there was little ammunition – many did not have the 150 rounds they should have been issued with – and there was precious little fresh water. Many men who survived the initial onslaught quickly fell to disease in the blistering heat.

The badge for the Dublin Fusiliers Royal Association.

GREAT IRISH HEROES

Some men met their deaths throwing rocks at the well-armed Turks. And the youth of Dublin paid the penalty *for* the huge blunder along with thousands of Australian and New Zealand casualties.

Many historians believe Irish units were cruelly used as cannon fodder by Churchill. Keith Murdoch, then a 29-year-old Australian war reporter, played a decisive role in forcing Churchill to call off the slaughter. The father of Rupert Murdoch, owner of the *Irish News of the World*, was horrified by what he witnessed. On his return from the frontline, he sent a letter to the Australian Prime Minister sharply criticising what was happening at Gallipoli. He was appalled by the carnage in an operation that men knew was a hopeless cause that had already claimed the lives of around 12,000 Australian and New Zealand soldiers. And with fellow journalists he started a campaign for the withdrawal of the troops. He won over many powerful people and on December 12, 1915, the withdrawal of the crushed invaders began.

Military planners were later condemned for their stupidity, but shrugged away blame. It was in the grieving backstreet homes of Dublin that the price was once again paid by the Irish.

The Royal Dublin Fusiliers Association website is at www.greatwar.ie

JOHN 'DAGGER' HUGHES

The Irish Bishop who tamed the gangs of New York

The struggles of 19th-century Irish emigrants to America are recounted in the acclaimed Martin Scorcese film *Gangs Of New York*. But the exploits of the bold fictional Irishman played by Leonardo DiCaprio are dwarfed by those of a real hero of those turbulent times.

Meet tough Archbishop John 'Dagger' Hughes of New York, once a starving, barefoot lad from the fields of Co. Tyrone. He became a true champion and saviour to his flock of thousands, and he tamed ranting killer mobs with powerful words and prayers that stifled mindless savagery. Alone, he faced entrenched hatred of Catholics on behalf of souls seeking only religious freedom and to break from poverty.

Screen idol DiCaprio plays Amsterdam Vallon in

In the film dramatisation of events, Daniel Day Lewis plays the gang leader 'Bill the Butcher'.

Liam Neeson plays Priest Vallon in the movie 'Gangs of New York'.

Scorsese's raw and disturbing movie. It tells of decades of foul and rampant sectarianism and brutality faced by Irish folk settling in America after years of oppression and the famine back home.

Dagger John – he got the name from the type of crucifix he wore – became a living legend in Irish-American history for standing up for justice. His finest moment came in 1863 when riots gripped New York and the name of the Irish was being dragged through the mud. Rival gangs had claimed the lives of more than 1,000 and parts of the city were razed by fire. Dagger John told gang leaders face to face that he could no longer allow death and destruction to reign and property to be torched. They heeded his powerful words. Within hours the madness stopped.

John Hughes was born into rural poverty in Ireland in

1797. He grew up in the bitter time of the penal laws, which had been brutally imposed on the Catholic population. His steely resolve to fight for Irish rights was forged one dark day when his sister died. He was just 15. In those days it was illegal under the British Penal Laws to allow a Catholic priest inside the church grounds. So the priest was forced to stand outside the church walls while John's sister was lowered into the ground without a proper burial. This sense of injustice would never leave John.

With no education, no rights to buy land and barely even the right to survive, John's family decided to take their chances in America. Later in life John recalled his excitement at going, and what he thought would allow his family a new life free from hate. 'A country in which no stigma of inferiority would be impressed on my brow,

Leonardo DiCaprio in the film.

simply because I professed one creed or another,' he said.

In 1817 the family set sail from Dublin harbour. John took a job labouring in the gardens of a seminary in Emmitsburg, Maryland. He talked to clerics and realised he had a calling for the religious way of life. He entered the priesthood in September, 1820, and after he qualified he was sent to the city of brotherly love, Philadelphia, for his first assignment.

But the city of love was not that welcoming to the Catholic population which had been steadily settling in. Here the rising young priest saw for the first time, outside the comfort of the seminary, that the reality in this new land of freedom mirrored much of the reality from back home. Being unskilled and uneducated, the Irish in America became the victims of Protestant ruling-class disdain and hatred for what they termed 'Pope lovers'.

John then set about to change this opinion of the Irish Catholics in the city with a massive campaign, which included a letter sent to all the major papers condemning the political leaders for their anti-Irish sentiments. In 1842, the then Bishop of New York, John Dubois, died and the young, energetic priest of Philadelphia was given his job in 1844.

Irish immigrants now flooded into the slums of notorious Five Points, New York, in search of a better life. Hughes fought to break the control of a few rich Catholics who were on the New York board of trustees and were taking offence at how he ran his diocese. He compared the trustees to the British and their unspeakable treatment of poor immigrant Catholics. At

121

The Archbishop John 'Dagger' Hughes who fought for Catholics in America.

the end of the speech the crowd were left weeping and he admitted that he, too, was almost moved to tears. 'I was not far from crying myself,' he said. Now the Irish of New York had someone who would fight for them and make sure they would not be treated like second-class citizens.

But after his first fight he was ready for another struggle in the public school system in New York, which only

The imposing front of St Patrick's Cathedral in New York.

taught the protestant faith. After a two-year battle the state legislature abolished the rule and the Irish celebrated in the streets of New York, hailing their archbishop as a hero.

In 1844, during anti-Catholic riots in Philadelphia, his former parish, two churches were burned down and 12 Catholics killed. These anti-Catholics threatened to do the same in New York. But Dagger John put armed guards around his churches and warned the New York mayor, 'If a single Catholic church is burned in New York, the city will be a second Moscow.' (The city of Moscow was burned to the ground by its citizens to prevent Napoleon from using it as winter quarters for his army).

The threat was taken seriously and an anti-Catholic march planned for the city was cancelled. Dagger John was now seen as a beacon to the Irish, who had for the first time a member of the clergy in America who was standing up for their poor and working class in the ghettos of their newly-adopted country.

Beginning in 1845, two million Irish emigrants fled Ireland from the potato famine over the next few years. This shocked him and he knew he would have to put all his efforts into helping his fellow countrymen as they came from the horrors of a dying land. Heartbroken, he wrote of the scene as starving Irish people disembarked from the coffin ships in their thousands: 'The utter destitution in which they reach these shores is almost inconceivable.'

Dagger John now launched a campaign to educate the uneducated and to preach to the Irish immigrants, who he hoped would not go looking for answers in the bottle. The Irish were then living in squalid conditions but the next generation would turn a devastated community into the future leaders of New York. With one great leap the Irish went from being reviled to being the pillars of the community. They became the judges and the lawyers, the teachers and also the political leaders.

In his final act of heroism in 1863, he broke up the infamous riots. He died on January 3, 1864, and on his deathbed spoke of his life and work being futile. But he left a legacy that would allow the Irish in their millions to thrive and their descendants to become Presidents.

Ironically, in the film, DiCaprio's character's father is an Irish priest who is murdered. But sadly producers did not see fit to mention the real Irish clerical hero of the era – Dagger John.

GREAT IRISH HERO
ROBERT EMMET

Robert's short but dramatic life came to a close when he was executed for treason in 1803 while trying to free Ireland. He left a noble mark on Irish history.

THE IRISH SOLDIERS
WHO DIED IN SPAIN

Ireland's other civil war

The ideological maelstrom of Ireland's Civil War was to be cruelly repeated – in Spain. The bitterness of the home-front divide took more than 3,000 lives in 1922. In 1936 legions of Irishmen joined sides in the Spanish Civil War to fight the same battles of faith and passion all over again. More than 300 were killed, hundreds more were maimed, and none escaped jarred minds and mental scars of the savagery. A cruel chapter for the history books pitted brother against brother and father against son in trenches in a foreign land. For the Irish there were no victors.

A Dublin historian said, 'It was a terrible tragedy that Irish soldiers were once again fighting against each other, and this time in a foreign land.'

Around 2,000 men took boats to Spain in organised

Father Michael O'Flanagan.

groups. Many more, either singly or in small parties, joined the conflict.

The seeds to the Spanish Civil War (1936–39) were sown in 1931 when monarchist candidates were voted out and a republic was proclaimed. The cruel rule of a wealthy elite backed up by brutal military police was over – for a while. People looked for land reform and an end to poverty, illiteracy and malnutrition.

By 1936, Spain was entering a bloody chapter in its history as Fascist leader General Franco led a revolt against the Republican government. He was backed by Hitler's Germany and Italy. Little did people know at the time how devastating this war would turn out to be for the whole of Europe. The Republican government had been strongly opposed by the middle classes and Catholic Church of Spain who saw them as anti-Catholic Communists in the grip of Russia.

Franco's group, known as the Nationalists, had their stronghold in the Spanish colonies of Africa from where they launched their offensive on the Spanish mainland. The conflict became truly international when Hitler unleashed the German air force on left-wing supporters. Nazi planes transported Franco's men to battle. Italy sent tanks, warplanes and 47,000 men, and the German Luftwaffe carried out its first blitzkrieg, using Stuka dive bombers to bomb civilians and obliterate the town Guernica.

Russia replied in kind, supporting the Republican government with arms and financial aid to conduct the war. It was now a battle between two ideologies, Fascism on one side and Communism on the other.

In Ireland, the bitter political divide over Spain became a cause. But the realities of war soon ruined the romantic notions of the young men as the Spanish Civil War turned into a bloody conflict. The backdrop was an Ireland where rebellion was in the air as the Blueshirts led by charismatic Eoin O'Duffy clamoured for a right-wing coup of Dail Eireann.

O'Duffy was a former commander of the IRA and Commissioner of the Gardai until 1933 when President de Valera, shocked by his Fascist beliefs and admiration of Hitler, sacked him from his post. O'Duffy, one of the founding members of Fine Gael, now began to attack his former comrades-in-arms. He made countless attacks on the IRA, infuriating leaders of the organisation by calling them Communists. This led to pitched battles between the two groups as tensions spilt over into the streets of 30s Ireland.

O'Duffy saw that the perfect battle ground for his Nazi-style Blueshirts would be in Spain and he began to recruit volunteers under his command to fight in the bitter war on the side of Franco. Left-wing parties in Ireland along with many IRA volunteers now began to recruit for what they saw as the socialist and democratically elected Republican government, which needed to be defended against the Fascists. So they set sail for Spain believing their cause to be right to the point where they would lay down their lives.

O'Duffy and his 750 men became part of the XV Bandera Irlandesa del Terico of the Spanish Foreign Legion. Survivors claimed after the war that they had

Eoin O'Duffy, former commander of the IRA and who later turned on them.

General Franco.

simply gone to defend the Catholic faith and not in support of Fascism.

In 1937, a Republican brigade surrounded Duffy and his men at a town called Jarama. The Irish battalion suffered huge losses as they were shelled unmercifully. More than 30 were killed and 250 badly injured. O'Duffy then issued a statement on why the Irish Brigade was leaving Spain. He said, 'My men have now been in front-line trenches for three months without a break. It has been a baptism of fire. They have been subjected to almost unceasing shell-fire and bombing day after day, night after night. We have many dead and many seriously wounded, some maimed for life. Many others are suffering from shellshock, pulmonary diseases, rheumatic fever developed during weeks of torrential

132

rain.' He spoke of a lack of drinking water and the onset of typhoid.

The passing of the Free State Non-Intervention Act in Ireland forbidding men and women from fighting overseas meant that there was no more support from home for fighters. O'Duffy said, 'No further support from Ireland will be forthcoming. The Irish post offices have even refused to accept parcels addressed to members of the brigade in Spain since the passing of the Act.' So the remnants of O'Duffy's little army called it a day in late 1937 and struggled home.

Survivors later told of being annoyed by falsehoods about why men went to Spain to fight. Everyone who joined O'Duffy was not a Fascist. The majority who fought for Franco had no interest in Fascism and were traditional Catholics. They did what they did because the Church told them to.

The Irish volunteers who had joined up with the International Socialists Brigade on the side of the Republicans were fairing no better than their bitter rivals. The Irish International Brigade was made up of trade union leaders and IRA volunteers representing all walks of life in Ireland. They put up with unimaginable hardships as Hitler's planes supported Franco by bombarding the Irish forces in a new type of war from the air that the world had not witnessed before. They participated in the defence of Madrid, which was a stronghold of the Republican forces. The volunteers witnessed death rain down from the skies daily in the form of Stuka dive bombers. They never forgot the

133

horror of what they saw as Madrid was wrecked by the relentless onslaught.

One Irish volunteer who fought hard in the chaos of Madrid remembers sending a telegram to his mother and father in his native Cork as he recovered from serious wounds. He said, 'I felt bad about the worry I had put them through and I sent a telegram to tell them I was OK.' Later, he came to realise that in certain quarters in his homeland he was seen as a traitor. The postman who delivered the telegram spat out these words to his mother: 'It's dead he should be, fighting against Christ.'

But there were still men in the Church willing to speak out in favour of the Irishmen who had gone to battle for socialism and the Republicans. One such man was the

Franco's fighters in action against the International Brigades. Irish soldiers fought on both sides of the bloody Spanish civil war.

Irish Republican priest, Father Michael O'Flanagan, who could not be silenced. He said, 'The fight in Spain is a fight between the rich, privileged classes and the rank and file of the poor, oppressed people of Spain.'

O'Duffy would die in 1944 and receive a full State funeral but history has recorded him as a Nazi who trained his men to give him Nazi salutes.

The Irish on the Republican side would continue their fight until the eventual defeat of the socialist forces of Spain by Franco's forces in 1939. He ruled Spain with an iron hand until his death in 1975.

The war in Spain would leave many remembering Irishmen on both sides for their bravery and humanity in the face of the sheer horrors of war. But, ironically, while the rest of the world marched off to the Second World War, Ireland entered a time of peace that had escaped it for generations.

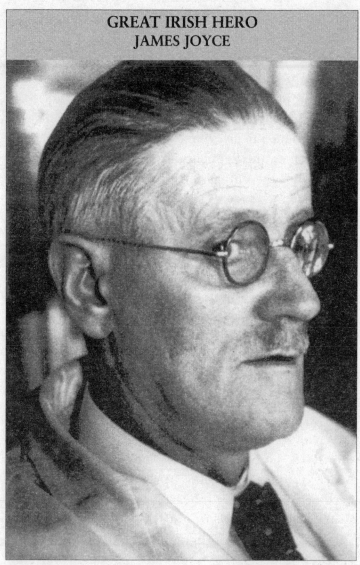

GREAT IRISH HERO
JAMES JOYCE

One of the greatest writers of the 20th century, Joyce produced a string of celebrated classics. He famously set his best-loved novel Ulysses in his home streets of Dublin.

ROBERT BLAIR MAYNE

**Irish rugby star joined SAS
to tackle Hitler**

Upper-crust snobs sneered when Robert Blair Mayne volunteered to be an army officer. Haughty Belfast University Officer Training Corps pen-pushers looked down their noses, doubted his soldiering ability and turned him away. They could not have made a more monumental blunder.

Within four years, burly Irishman Mayne, 23, a rugby international, had joined the bravest of the brave with the Allies' 1st Special Air Service Regiment in North Africa during the Second World War. He went on to become commanding officer of the elite regiment that struck German airfields and fuel dumps at night. He rose to the rank of lieutenant-colonel and won a chestful of medals. He would have had many more but he always played down his astonishing exploits and asked his men not to talk about them.

137

An older Robert Blair Mayne.

To this day Mayne's deeds take pride of place in the history of the SAS at their HQ in Hereford, England. Using incendiary bombs, Mayne is credited with destroying more than 100 German warplanes and dozens of other targets. Hitler ordered SAS men to be shot on sight because of their amazing exploits.

Historians say Mayne played a key role in helping bring the Germans to their knees in the bloody conflict across North Africa in 1942 and hampered Rommel's feared Afrika Korps. One said, 'Only now is the importance of his contribution to the victory of the Allies in North Africa becoming fully understood.'

Mayne's daring operations in Jeeps armed with machine guns bordered on the lunatic, For capture often meant torture and execution. Mayne and his men drove to

Special Air Service Regiment founder David Stirling, right, with his men ready to set off on a raid behind German lines.

By the end of his career, Paddy Mayne was a highly decorated man.

within striking distance of airfields and camps. With stealth and derring-do, they attached incendiary devices to German planes and fuel supplies, and often fled under heavy rifle-fire.

During one raid Mayne ran out of bombs to plant on parked Messerschmitt 109 fighter planes. Five were already alight, So he used his bare hands to attack and wreck the cockpit controls of the sixth. He dodged safely into the darkness as German sentries fired on him and a group of his men.

Another deadly ploy used by Mayne was to send a squadron of Jeeps armed with heavy machine guns racing through German airfields and bases – often under fire – destroying planes and supplies.

Scot David Stirling, the founder and commander of the SAS, was captured and sent to the infamous Colditz Castle as a prisoner for the rest of the war. Mayne then took command and he ran the regiment with great skill until the end of the war.

Robert Blair Mayne was born on January 11, 1915, at the family home in Mountpleasant, Newtownards, Co. Down. He was the second youngest child in a family of seven – four boys and three girls – and was named after his mother's cousin, Robert Blair, who was awarded the Distinguished Service Order in 1915 for rescuing fellow soldiers while under heavy German fire in the First World War.

Young Robert's thoughts at first were not of being a hero on the battlefield but conquering the sports field. He was a dedicated rugby player in his early days for his local club Ards RFC. Paddy Blair, as he was known, later

141

studied at Queen's University, Belfast, where he continued playing rugby and also took up boxing, at which he went on to become the Irish Universities' Heavyweight Champion.

A university friend at the time said, 'I remember Queen's being fairly rough in those days. Blair was not gratuitously violent. However, with his size, strength, timing and ability it was inevitable that he would join the boxing club.'

However, it was rugby that was his main passion and he gained a host of honours on the field including six Irish caps and playing for the British Lions on their tour of South Africa in 1938. But before he could hit the big time in his rugby career, war clouds gathered over Europe and spelled the end of his playing days.

The stupidity of the Officer Training Corps at Queen's did not deter Mayne. But their derogatory words about his aptitude always stayed with him.

Burly, energetic Mayne was determined to be a soldier and join the fight to rid the world of the scourge of Hitler. He joined his local unit, the 5th Light Anti-Aircraft Battery. Later he transferred to various other units, including the Royal Ulster Rifles and the Cameronians before seeing his first action with the 11 Commando. It was then that he came to the attention of David Stirling.

The first mission Mayne undertook for the SAS was in 1942 in North Africa. It was a disaster – 66 men were parachuted behind enemy lines and only 22 survived. So Stirling turned to Jeeps for greater mobility for his raiders. The effect was devastating. German losses to the SAS and

A rare wartime picture of Paddy Mayne, a natural leader.

Mayne not only played rugby for Ireland but was a boxing champ as well.

their pals in the Long Range Desert Group were so great that Hitler ordered thousands of troops due to be sent to France to stay in North Africa to combat the menace. Mayne's reputation as a ferocious and fearless fighter grew. Somehow his name was known to the Germans. The historian added, 'After a while word of Paddy's actions made it to the highest ranks of the German Reich. Hitler issued an order of shoot to kill, describing Paddy and his band of warriors as dangerous men.'

Mayne was once asked about his success and replied, 'When you burst into a hut full of enemy soldiers you must remember the drill involved for such occasions. Shoot the first person who makes a move, hostile or otherwise. His brain has recovered from the shock of seeing you there with a gun. He has started to think and there is the danger.'

A fellow SAS officer said, 'Out of battle, he was a most gentle, kind man who possessed all the qualities of leadership. He had an ingenious brain which was always seeking new ways to harry the enemy.' Paddy fought all the way to Germany with the SAS, never relenting and with a steely determination to see the war come to an end.

Paddy returned to his hometown and settled down to a peacetime life. But after years of surviving the most incredible wartime dangers, he was killed in a car crash in 1955 a few hundred yards from his home. In his town of Newtownards stands a statue of Robert Blair Mayne. It is larger than life. Just like the great man himself.

GREAT IRISH HERO
PADRAIG PEARSE

Self-taught Irish speaker Pearse became an IRA leader. He left his profession of teaching and in 1916 led a revolt on the GPO. He was arrested and executed after their defeat by Crown Forces.

CHAIM HERZOG

Irish Hero who trapped Himmler

The quick-witted Irish interrogator was only momentarily fooled by the cringing, sallow-faced German across the table. The slight and scruffy man claimed to be a humble SS sergeant without a stain of wartime guilt. But British army chief intelligence officer Major Chaim Herzog was not thrown off the scent by the man's eye patch, attempts to change his appearance and the name Heinrich Hitzinger. Recognition of the face suddenly rushed to the front of Chaim's mind. Sitting opposite him in the cold, bare prison-camp room was, in fact, Heinrich Himmler, the dreaded and powerful Nazi leader second in evil only to Adolf Hitler.

Himmler, the maniac who plotted the Final Solution to wipe out the Jewish race, was finally trapped by the son of

Chaim Herzog displays happiness at becoming president of Israel.

the Chief Rabbi of Ireland who was raised in Dublin and went on to become the sixth President of Israel. The interrogation that snared the Gestapo mass-murderer happened in April 1945 as he made a bid to skulk away to Switzerland and his looted gold hoard. But 45-year-old Himmler never faced his war crimes accusers and certain execution. A month later he bit on a cyanide pill given to all high-ranking Germans and died in agony within minutes.

As Himmler rotted in Hell, Chaim Herzog led a distinguished life as a dedicated and eloquent champion of all Jewish people until his death in 1997. He was born into an Irish-Jewish family in Belfast and moved to Dublin in 1931 for most of his schooling at Wesley College, a breeding ground for many famous Irish figures. His father, Rabbi Yitzak HaLevi Herzog, served the needs of a growing Jewish population who fled the Nazi persecution spreading across Europe.

Chaim left Ireland for Palestine in 1935 at the age of 17 when his father became Chief Rabbi to Middle East Jews. Sorrow at the thought of leaving Ireland was tempered by the excitement of reaching the Jewish homeland. He studied law in the Talmudic Academy but the drum-beats of war began to sound in Nazi Germany. Before he could turn his attention to his native Europe the scholarly Chaim turned to the fight in his new country.

A newly formed group of Jewish revolutionaries called the Haganah persuaded him to throw his books down and take up the gun during the Arab revolt from 1936–39. The teenager had now turned into a man with his first

Chaim with the US stateman Colin Powell.

taste of war, which would become familiar to him as the world entered turbulent times.

He returned to his studies and headed for England to further his education. While in London, the fog of war descended on Europe as Hitler's madness plunged the continent into darkness.

The young idealist was not about to turn his gaze away from the sufferings he knew were happening in Europe to his fellow Jews. He marched into a British army recruiting office and signed on to fight for five years.

Officers saw that this quick-witted young man had something to offer other than being just a soldier. He was reassigned as an intelligence officer and that posting threw him headlong into the dangers of occupied Europe. He headed to Normandy when the Allies invaded and later to Belgium, showing his bravery in collecting intelligence and hunting down Nazi leaders. He made history by being one of the first into occupied Germany after having fought his way across Europe. But his dream of seeing the defeat of Hitler would turn into a nightmare one morning when he and fellow soldiers liberated the notorious death camp Bergen-Belsen.

There, to his horror, he discovered the appalling depths

Chaim with his wife Aura and their children.

Chaim meets Britain's Queen during a state visit.

of depravity to which man can sink. He was sickened by the stench of death. Generations of Jewish families lay dead on the frozen grounds of Belsen. They had been gassed in Himmler's death chambers.

Chaim Herzog was determined to avenge them. After the fall of Germany in 1945 Nazi leaders went on the run. It was then, as he interviewed captured German soldiers, that he realised he had Himmler at bay. He knew that this man's face and story did not match up.

Chaim stayed on in Germany as a chief military intelligence officer having left the British army with the rank of lieutenant-colonel, then in 1947 he returned to Palestine to join the intelligence service there. In 1948, as what was left of Europe's Jews fled to the Middle East and the promise of a new life, he served in the Haganah, the Jewish underground which became the Israel Defence Force in 1948 when the State of Israel was created following the War of Independence. He was the commander of an armoured brigade and a master tactician fighting tank battles.

Chaim was one of the fathers of Moss ad, the crack Israeli intelligence unit that hunted down Nazis and enemies of the State with a ruthlessness that earned it respect throughout the world. He retired from the Israeli army in 1962 with the rank of major-general.

Over the next two decades Chaim combined an extensive business career, first as managing director of an industrial development group and later as a senior partner in a Tel Aviv law firm, with public service. He was chief military commentator for Israel Radio during both

Himmler, the man who was fundamental in crafting the Final Solution.

the Six-Day War and the Yom Kippur War. His broadcasts boosted the morale of the population and raised his standing with the Israeli people even further. He was called back to active duty after the 1967 Six-Day War to serve as the first military governor of Judea, Samaria and East Jerusalem.

His skill as a statesman came to the fore during the three tough years from 1975 when he was Israel's ambassador to the UN. A hostile coalition of the Communist bloc and Arab countries tried to equate Zionism with racism. Chaim publicly tore up the draft resolution as he defended his country's right to survive.

He wrote many books on Israeli military history and was always a much sought-after commentator on political and military affairs, but still found time to be a dedicated family man with three children.

In 1981 he was elected a member of the Knesset, the Israeli parliament, and quickly came to prominence in the ruling Labour Party. Then, in 1983, came his proudest achievement – he was elected as the country's sixth President, a post he held for 10 years. As President he travelled widely with the aim of enhancing Israel's standing in the world. He made State visits to more than 30 countries. He made the first visits by an Israeli President to Germany and China. He also made an historic trip of reconciliation to Spain, marking 500 years since the expulsion of the Jews.

Urbane and frank, Herzog always challenged criticism of his country and pushed trade deals that allowed Israel to prosper. And he fought for the Israeli nation to help

Jewish people throughout the world. He campaigned for Jewish people to be allowed to leave Communist Russia.

In 1985 he made an official visit back to his beloved Ireland, the first time he had returned since his youth. In an emotional ceremony he opened the Jewish Museum in Dublin to remember the thousands of Jews who had made Ireland their home. He met many old friends and people who knew him as a lad. Many of them told him they always knew he was destined for greatness.

In 1993 he stepped down as President of Israel but continued to pursue his passion of helping Jews throughout the world. He carried on writing and speaking up for Israel. And he often mentioned that being raised in Ireland had given him a real taste for fairness and justice.

He passed away peacefully in 1997 and received a full Israeli State funeral for his services to Jewish people. Chaim Herzog was a true leader. And a true hero.

EDWARD 'MICK' MANNOCK

The Irish hero who was the greatest fighter ace of them all

One of the most astounding secrets of World War I is that Britain's top gun was Irish.

Edward 'Mick' Mannock was credited with 73 'kills' – shooting down German planes – making him *the* leading Brit air force fighter pilot of the Great War.

His glory trail came to an abrupt end when anti-aircraft fire sent him spinning to his death over Lille, France, on July 26, 1918. But the memory of the 31-year-old hero lives on both in military history and in his birthplace of Ballincollig, Co. Cork.

Captain WE Johns, a Royal Flying Corps pilot who later wrote the classic Biggles tales, said of Mick, 'Irish by birth, he displayed all the impetuosity of the Irish. He was, of course, a fearless fighter. He was also a brilliant leader and exponent of the air combat tactics of his time.'

British military chiefs recorded that Mick was born in Aldershot, England. But, in fact, his Catholic parents lived in Ireland when Mick first drew breath on May 24, 1887. Dad Edward was a hard-drinking corporal in the British army, who abandoned the family when Mick was 12. Mum Julia then moved with Mick to Wellingborough, Northamptonshire, to start a new life. His father's desertion instilled a toughness in the young Mick that would serve him well later on in life. But as a boy, Mick had no desire to follow in his father's footsteps and join the armed forces.

By 1911, Mick was working as a post office engineer in Wellingborough – a good job for an Irish working-class lad at the time. Then in February, 1914, he was sent to Turkey to lay cable lines for the post office there. It proved to be the turning point in his life. For on November 2, 1914, Turkey allied itself with Germany and entered the war against Britain and France.

Mick was interned and treated brutally by the Turks, even though he was not in the military. The pain and suffering quickly developed into a deep-seated hatred of the Turks and Germans. Mick's determination to get revenge looked like a lost cause as the terrible treatment sent his health plummeting. But then in 1915, the Turks – believing Mick was at death's door – repatriated him under a deal with the British. It would turn out to be a massive blunder by the Turkish authorities. The following year, after the young Irishman had recovered his strength, he joined the British forces to wreak his revenge.

Mick quickly gained a commission in the Royal

Mick Mannock, ace pilot and WWI hero.

Engineers' Signal section, which was quite a feat for a self-educated Irishman in the class-conscious British army of the day. But Mick was not content with this posting and applied for his ultimate dream of being a pilot in the newly formed flying squadrons.

His dream came true on March 31, 1917, when he was accepted and sent to join 40 Squadron on the Western Front, where the bloodiest battles of the war were taking place.

WWI air battle in progress.

One of his new comrades wrote of him, 'He seemed a know-all and we felt the quicker he got amongst the Huns, the better that would show him how little he knew.'

They were right. When Mick was sent up for his first encounter with the enemy, he panicked. But it only served to make him all the more determined and from that point on, he sat down to learn the art of dog-fighting. On June 17, 1917, Mick scored his first kill and the legend of the ace pilot was born. His killing prowess continued, sending plane after plane plummeting from the skies in balls of flames. Before long, Mick was awarded the Military Cross and promoted to acting captain and flight commander.

Under Mick's command was another Irish fighting ace George McElroy, who earned both the Distinguished Flying Cross and Military Cross. George came from Donnybrook, Dublin, and had transferred from the Royal Irish Regiment.

They became good friends, sharing the common bond of being the Irishmen in the squadron. But time was not on their side and George was shot down a few days after Mick clocked up his 46th kill. Mick locked the pain inside and got on with his job. He was later given 30 days' leave but after a couple of days away from the airfield and his men, he was itching to get back into the action.

In one incident, he was put in charge of a training squadron and famously led them to attack a rival HQ, dropping 200 oranges on it. But the next day they were bombed in a retaliatory strike with 200 bananas.

When he returned to the war in France, Mick found another Irish pilot had joined his squadron. Dubliner

Henry Dolan was one of his most promising pilots. But in May, 1918, he was shot down. This time Mick was unable to hide his emotions and went on a drinking spree. His friends were now being killed on a daily basis.

James McCudden, only 22 years old, who was born in Kent to Irish parents, was killed on July 9, 1918, with 51 kills to his name. Mick was devastated and went on a week of rampage and destruction. He wrote his last letter home and in it he sounds like a man destroyed by war. 'I feel that life is not worth hanging on to – had hopes of getting married but …' was all the soul-destroyed man could say.

On July 26, 1918, Mick set out with trainee Irish-New Zealander Lieutenant Donald Inglis on a routine patrol. They encountered and destroyed two German aircraft. Inglis describes what happened next: 'Falling in behind Mick again, we made a couple of circles around the burning wreck of the second German aircraft and then made for home. I saw Mick start to kick his rudder. His nose dropped slightly and he went into a slow right-hand turn and hit the ground in a burst of flames. I circled at about 20 feet but could not see him. As things were getting hot, I made for home and managed to reach our outposts with a punctured fuel tank. Poor Mick – the bloody bastards had shot my major down in flames.' It is believed that Mick's plane was hit by freak anti-aircraft fire.

Mick was known by his fellow pilots as an Irish nationalist proud of his roots. Yet, as one history expert sums up, 'Few other people ever realised that he was, in fact, Irish.'

GREAT IRISH HERO
JIM LARKIN

Labour leader Larkin became a hero to the masses in 1909 when he helped Irish workers get better pay and conditions. He died penniless having given everything for the struggle of the working man.

JOHN McCORMACK

**The Irish tenor who was the
first world pop star**

Long before the likes of U2 and the Corrs were even born, a talented Irishman became the first singer to achieve international fame. Legendary crooner Count John McCormack wowed millions across the globe with his good looks and soaring voice. The Irish singer was born into an impoverished family of eleven in Athlone, Co. Westmeath, on June 14, 1884. From these humble beginnings he went on to cause a sensation throughout the world.

His talent was first noticed in his early teens when one of his schoolteachers asked him to sing in front of a visiting dignitary, who was stunned by the youngster's rich voice. Modest McCormack later recalled, 'I had an absolute fear of singing but I also had a sense of wanting to sing the song well and I think they liked it.' From that

McCormack in passionate performance.

moment the budding star was determined to get into the music industry. 'The singing spirit must have been there. Like the man born to be hanged, I was born to sing,' he later said.

But his dream was opposed by his father, Andrew McCormack, who wanted his children to have 'respectable' professions. At one stage Andrew even pushed his golden-voiced son towards the priesthood. The determined youngster resisted and signed up to the prestigious Palestrina Choir at the Pro-Cathedral in Dublin. There his formidable singing talent was lovingly nurtured.

McCormack was a dedicated student and would practice his vocal ranges late into the night until he was satisfied his performance was perfect. His hard work was rewarded in 1903 at the age of 19 when he entered Feis Ceoil, Ireland's premier musical competition, in Dublin.

The unknown Athlone lad was the last contestant to perform and was not expected to win. But his amazing voice worked the crowds into a frenzy, securing a glorious victory. The audience was screaming and cheering so loudly that the judges were unable even to announce the result. One judge finally shouted, 'You have shown by your applause that you have made my decision for us and you are quite right.'

With both his profile and confidence boosted, McCormack set off for the US, where he had lined up a string of concerts. But the fiery Irishman was furious when he saw the warm-up act intended to accompany his performances – a comedian who played a drunken Irish fool. Patriotic McCormack cornered the promoter and demanded, 'Either me or the comedian.' Unfortunately for McCormack, the promoter chose the comedian and he had to pack his bags.

The singer returned to Ireland, where he met his future wife, Lily Foley, a fellow singer whom he wed in 1906. The pair went on to have two children, Cyril and Gwen.

Shortly after his marriage, McCormack decided to turn his hand to opera and headed over to Italy to star in *Mascagni's L'Amico Fritz*. Under the name of Giovanni Foli, he wowed audiences in the title role of a man twice his age. The talented performer went on to earn similar success in England in the opera *Cavalleria Rusticana* in London's Covent Garden in 1907. But after performing further operatic roles, McCormack realised his acting would never match up to his singing and left the theatre to pursue his true vocation.

Despite his musical talent, his career in England began to flounder as a result of his outspoken support of Irish nationalism. He decided to head once again for American shores, where he quickly won a large following.

In 1918, shortly after the end of World War I, McCormack was stunned to receive an invitation to sing for American President Woodrow Wilson and selected guests at a State dinner. Fresh from this honour, he became an American citizen in 1919. But loyal McCormack never forgot Ireland and frequently returned to his beloved home country and its musical heritage. He once said, 'First, I give people the songs they want to hear, then I give them the songs they ought to like and, thirdly, I give them the songs of my native land – which are truly the most beautiful.'

McCormack with his wife Lily and children Cyril and Gwen.

Ahead of his time and always aware of his roots: John McCormack.

McCormack's fame spread around the world as he concentrated on recording gramophone records, having made his first in 1904, to bring his music into people's homes. His smooth voice, coupled with his handsome looks, won him global adoration on a scale comparable to that won by The Beatles decades later. Like the fab four, McCormack was ahead of his time and was not afraid to defy the critics, many of whom called his music unsophisticated and popularist. He argued, 'People of all classes have a perfect right to enjoy music.'

In 1928 McCormack, a dedicated Catholic, achieved a lifelong dream when he was named a count of the Knights of Columbus by the Pope, a title he proudly appended to his name on his concert programmes. In the same year he made his one and only film, a musical called *Song O'My Heart*. With this achievement and the knowledge that he had played a major role in creating the record market, McCormack felt confident enough to have another try at winning fame in Britain. This time he was given a warm welcome and performed sell-out concerts to thousands across the country. He continued to tour throughout the world and to record more songs, mainly for HMV Records. McCormack made his last record in 1942 at the age of 58. The musical legend then broadcast and played occasional concerts for one more year before failing health forced him to retire.

During his 40-year career McCormack recorded some of the most famous hits of all time, including 'It's A Long Way To Tipperary' and 'When Irish Eyes Are Smiling'.

The shining light of world music died in 1945, leaving a legacy of beautiful songs that future generations would also come to love. In his last words to the world – in memoirs discovered after his death – he said, 'I live again the days and evenings of my long career. I dream at night of operas and concerts in which I have had my share of success. Now, like the old Irish minstrels, I have hung up my harp because my songs are all sung.' But though Count McCormack is gone, he and his songs will never be forgotten.

GREAT IRISH HERO
GABRIEL BYRNE

Former star of RTE's Bracken show, Byrne has become one of the hottest names in Hollywood. But the hunky actor still returns to Dublin to unwind on a regular basis.

JIM CORBETT

**Ireland's gentleman champ who
taught the world to box clever**

Boxer 'gentleman' Jim Corbett gave the fighting
Irish of America a good name – for a change! In
many US cities, Irish immigrants had become a by-
word for violence and thuggery but stylish Corbett
was the epitome of civility. And the hearts of
impoverished Irish people swelled with pride as he
tackled opponents with a new style which took the
boxing world by storm.

James John Corbett was born in 1866 to Cork emigrant
parents shortly after they arrived in San Francisco. A
bright lad, he went to college and initially worked as a
bank clerk. In the evenings he would spar with top
boxers of the day in San Francisco's famed Olympic
Club. He was the first of a new breed of boxer, far
removed from the cauliflower-eared thugs who had held

173

Jim Corbett: a real gentleman.

sway in the ring until then and is credited as the 'Father of Modern Boxing'. Undoubtedly one of the greatest heavyweights of all time, he introduced a new era of 'science' fighting. He was described as clever, agile and 'jack-rabbit' quick. He used fast jabs and hooks, and possessed excellent footwork along with slippery head and body movements.

Because of his good looks and classy boxing style he earned several nicknames such as 'Handsome' Jim and 'Pompadour' Jim until one, 'Gentleman' Jim, finally stuck.

Fellow boxers and fans fell under the spell of the affable young contender who became respected by opponents and idolised by spectators. The public and boxing promoters were enthralled by his fighting style, which was so removed from that of the stereotypical brawling prize-fighter.

Corbett had a 23-bout five-year amateur boxing career and became the Olympic Club's middleweight champion and boxing instructor before turning professional aged 23 in 1889. He met the famed Joe Choynski who was known as the best fighter in boxing history never to gain a title. Corbett had previously fought Choynski in his first public amateur contest. They met three times in as many weeks in 1889. The first bout was a no-contest after four rounds and the police intervened, but Corbett won the second 27-round epic contest – fought on a barge – by a knockout. Corbett wore 2-oz gloves while Choynski wore skin gloves with seams. In the final fight Corbett outclassed Choynski in the fourth round with a knock-out.

Corbett's next titanic struggle, against hall-of-fame Peter

Depiction of fans carrying the champion, after he had beaten
John L Sullivan.

Corbett is considered by many to be the 'father' of modern boxing.

Corbett in his prime.

Jackson a year later, went to 61 bloody rounds over four hours and was finally declared a no-contest. But the Irish-American's record had set him on the road for the title fight of his life. A month later he had an inconclusive bout with fellow Irish-American John L Sullivan before meeting him again in the heavyweight championship of the world contest.

Sullivan was a living legend. His parents had emigrated from Co. Kerry to Boston around 1850 and John was born in 1858. Known as the 'Boston Strong Boy', Sullivan became a boxing immortal and the first great American sporting idol. He had been schooled in bare-knuckle fighting and is seen as the link between that and glove boxing. An old-fashioned slugger, he was also a hard drinker and bar-room brawler. Tough, powerful and quick, Sullivan could hit hard with both fists but had exceptional strength in his right. He could also take punishment and many consider him one of the best heavyweights ever. He enthralled the public with his ability to knock out opponents with ease.

Corbett and Sullivan would make history as they became the first opponents to fight for a world title under the Marquis of Queensbury rules. Apart from standard 50-oz gloves, there was no hitting below the belt and rounds were limited to three minutes. Defending his title, Sullivan was criticised in the pre-match hype for making Corbett fork up $10,000 for his chance to take on the former bare-knuckle bruiser. But Corbett rose to the challenge, for the winner would take a handsome $45,000 purse that would secure a life of luxury.

As the main event approached the excitement built among Irish fans across the nation, as people sided with their favourite boxer. On September 7, 1892, the talking stopped as 10,000 people packed the stadium in New Orleans to witness the two fighting Irish slug it out. They had each paid the then hefty sum of between $5 and $15 dollars a seat.

Sullivan, the 5ft 10in 33-year-old favourite at 4–1, weighed in at slightly more than 15st while the 6ft 1in 26-year-old challenger weighed in at just 12st 10lbs.

The decisive moment came in the third round when Corbett capitalised on Sullivan's weak defence and swung a deadly left hook to break the champion's nose! Corbett skipped around the ring showing off his new style of boxing, side-stepping and parrying the bloodied Sullivan's attacks. In the seventh round Corbett pummelled Sullivan who had no answer to the new boxing wizard. Finally, halfway through the 21st round, as Sullivan was tiring, Corbett unleashed a series of body blows forcing the champion on to the ropes. Sullivan sank to the canvas then staggered to his feet only to receive a withering one-two from Corbett which floored the former undefeated champion. Sullivan was counted out.

Gracious in defeat, Sullivan said, 'I came into the ring once too often and if I had to get licked I'm glad I was licked by a fellow Irish-American.'

Jim would go on to fight many more bouts but would never recapture the glory of that night in New Orleans which emblazoned his name in boxing history. He finally lost his crown in 1897 to another Irish-American, a fitter,

180

lighter Bob Fitzsimmons, one of a host of new fighters versed in the Gentleman Jim style of boxing.

Corbett died in New York in 1933 and, along with Sullivan and Fitzsimmons, was elected to the International Boxing Hall of Fame in 1990.

GREAT IRISH HERO
WOLFE TONE

One of Ireland's greatest patriots, Wolfe Tone planned a daring uprising involving French volunteers who he hoped would free Ireland. Sadly captured and facing certain death, he slit his own throat.

JOHN HOLLAND

How an Irish inventor's sub
went down in history

Deep beneath the waves the submarines of the
world's navies silently prowl the oceans … owing
their very existence to an Irishman's inventive brain.
For the father of all modem submarines is John
Holland, born more than a century and a half ago in a
small Co. Clare town.

Despite his humble beginnings Holland went on to
design and build the world's first submarine, from which
stem all of to day's mighty nuclear warships of the deep.
Yet his invention left him financially ruined and it was not
until many years after his death that John Philip Holland
was given due recognition for his revolutionary invention.

Born in 1841 at Liscannor, the young Holland was soon
to witness at firsthand the dreadful famine years and the
tragedy they brought. Although his father, also called

The submarine is tested off the American coast.

John, had a job as a coastguard – patrolling the coast on horseback – the family were still desperately poor. They managed to keep the famine from their door, but young John lost his father and his younger brother Robert, both killed by cholera in 1847.

His mother Mary moved with John and his two surviving brothers to Limerick and he first began to show his inventive mind when he began attending the Christian Brothers school in Ennistymon, Co. Clare. One Christian Brother in particular, Dominic Burke, took John under his wing and encouraged the youngster to develop his keen interest in science and mechanics.

John eventually opted to join the Christian Brothers himself, becoming a teacher in their schools while at the same time continuing to work on his ideas and inventions as a hobby. But while he was a schoolmaster in Cork an event happened 3,000 miles away off the coast of America that was to change the course of his life. For on March 9,

1862, during the American Civil War, the first naval battle took place between two all-metal ships – the *Monitor* from the Union and the Confederacy's *Merrimac*. Holland later revealed that when he learned news of the engagement, 'it struck me very forcibly that the day of wooden walls for vessels of war had passed, and that iron-clad ships had come to stay forever.'

It was then that he began thinking about the possibilities of metal ships that travelled underwater, but for a while he still busied himself with another machine he was trying to invent – the aeroplane.

The launch of the USS Holland.

Eventually his attention turned back to submarines. As he once said, 'The seed was implanted in my head but did not take root immediately.' So he taught children during the day while at night he designed the world's first submarine, coming up with his initial design in 1863. In the following years he continued to try to perfect his submarine designs but it was not until after he moved to the United States in 1873 that his quest began in earnest.

His younger brother Michael had already fled to America after being involved in the abortive Fenian rebellion of 1865–67, followed by his mother and brother leaving Ireland in 1872. John joined the family in Boston,

The ship's crew.

Holland inspects the conning tower of the USS Holland, the first
military submarine which he designed and built in the 1890s.

187

John Holland.

where they had set up home, the following year and quickly found backers for his submarine designs. But these were not the normal financiers one might expect. Instead his brother Michael introduced the young teacher to a band of American-based Fenians who agreed to finance the building of his designs in the hope could use them to plant explosives on docked British ships. However, after numerous disagreements, the Fenians stole his prototypes and as a result John decided to sever all contact with the revolutionary movement.

By 1883 Holland, now 42, had decided to quit his teaching career and move full time into building submarines. After getting backers for his ideas he set up The Holland Torpedo Company and in 1890 he entered a competition hoping to win a navy contract allowing him to build a new fleet of underwater warships. Unfortunately the competition was scrapped and he turned again to private funding for his ventures and built another ship, which would be known as *Holland VI*. By now he had developed the idea of neutral buoyancy – pumping water in and out of the vessel to balance it – and of using an engine and batteries for power.

The US navy decided to get involved at this point, realising the genius behind the design. Unfortunately for Holland, the building of the craft ruined him financially and the navy seized on this fact, buying the boat in 1900 for $150,000. It was only half its development cost but it allowed a desperate Holland to pay off his creditors. In the process, the Irish inventor forfeited the rights to his patent and on March 28, 1904 – after much wrangling between him and the money men – he resigned from the company he had started.

The US navy did at least name their boat in honour of the man that designed it, calling it the USS *Holland*. They also assigned a Number One to the hull of the craft, meaning that his name would go down in history as the first submarine designer for the US navy.

Armed with three torpedoes and a gun, the 54ft-long craft weighed 74 tons and had a crew of seven. Its design was soon copied by navies across the world, including in Great Britain and Japan, but Holland died in August, 1914, at the age of 73, shortly before submarines were tested in battle in the First World War.

'He died without recognition, until years later when he would be acknowledged as the father of the modem submarines,' said one history expert. But submarines proved their worth in the First World War and from then on became an essential part in any modem navy fleet's arsenal of weapons.

Today's nuclear-powered giants, armed with awesome cruise missiles, may seem a world away from the USS *Holland*, but they are still based on the same neutral buoyancy principles first laid down by the man from Co. Clare. And, in a touching tribute, his gravestone in New Jersey is etched with the thanks of sailors throughout the world for his work. It reads, 'John P Holland, Father of the modem submarine, dedicated by past, present and future submariners'.

GREAT IRISH HERO
GEORGE BEST

One of the greatest footballers ever, and one of the most loved despite his struggle with alcoholism.

BERNADO O'HIGGINS

Father of a nation

Heroic son of Ireland Bernardo O'Higgins made an astonishing mark on the world – founding a nation. To this day school textbooks across Chile teach children of his famed deeds and bravery. Statues and named landmarks in capital Santiago and across the country honour the free spirit of their champion O'Higgins. He led Chileans oppressed by Spanish rulers into countless battles that eventually won them freedom from the yoke of European monarchs. Ceremonies revere O'Higgins' name every September 18, commemorating Chile's Independence Day in 1810.

The story surrounding Bernardo began in 1720 when his father Ambrose was born the son of a peasant at Ballinary, Co. Sligo. Ambrose had little hope of a fruitful life under harsh English Protestant rule and,

A scene depicting the decisive 1818 Battle of Maipu.

like many young men, fled the country for advancement denied him at home. His uncle was a priest in Cadiz, Spain, and Ambrose stole aboard a ship to join him in his early 20s. Ambrose was trained as an engineer by the Jesuits and went to South America to work with the Spanish army. The quick-witted Irishman became a top administrator for the royalist regime. He planned towns and founded a postal service with Argentina across the Andes. Grateful Spanish leaders gave him the title of Baron de Ballenary.

At the age of 57 Ambrose fell for beautiful Isabel Riquelme, the voluptuous daughter of an aristocratic Santiago family. Sadly, they could not wed because European public officials were barred by law from marrying local women. But the couple's love still flowered and a year later in 1778 their illegitimate red-haired son

Born a peasant's son, Bernardo O'Higgins died a hero of the Chilean people.

Bernardo O'Higgins was born and a new chapter in the history of Chile was written.

Ambrose took good care of his son by making sure he was baptised and educated in Chile and England. Young Bernardo soaked up revolutionary ideas and took a ship to Spain, where he met Jose de San Martin who later liberated Argentina. Ambrose died in 1801 after trying to help the Chilean people he felt had been maltreated by the Spanish crowd. He left his wealth to Bernardo, who used it to help finance the freedom battle.

It was not until 1808 that Napoleon provided the chance needed when he invaded Spain and placed his brother Joseph on the Spanish throne, causing a bloody war between factions in Spain. Bernardo took the opportunity to seize power in September, 1810, and was elected to the Chilean National Congress. But royalists and those in favour of a breakaway state increasingly grew more hostile and civil war erupted.

Bernardo bankrolled an army of peasants and took command of two cavalry companies. His band of freedom fighters soon encountered the might of the Spanish royalists in the 1813 battle of Sorpresa del Roble in which he cried out to his men as he charged ranks of loyalists, 'Live with honour or die with glory. He who is brave, follow me.' In the battle he distinguished himself by leading a final charge, which led to victory for the peasants.

Bernardo became commander-in chief of the new Chilean army and went on to record more triumphs before reverses began. Against a superior army, Bernardo was forced to seek refuge in Argentina for three years. He trekked across the Andes with his followers and on April 5, 1818, he won the decisive battle of Maipu, now the heart of one of Chile's most famous wine growing areas. In six hours 2,000 Spanish soldiers were killed and 3,000 captured, compared with 1,000 Chilean losses.

Joyful Chileans made Bernardo their supreme ruler. He reorganised the country, setting up colleges, courts, libraries and hospitals. But his social reforms were too hasty for the Catholic hierarchy who saw their hold on the country slipping. In 1823 frustrated Bernardo resigned and left for exile in Peru, embittered by the politics of the Church and the wealthy. He died in Lima in 1842. But in 1866 his body was returned to Chile amid great ceremony as he was laid to rest in Santiago. He was a hero to his people.

GREAT IRISH HERO
BRENDAN BEHAN

Behan joined the IRA at 16 and went on to produce some of Ireland's classic plays, including The Quare Fellow. He was loved by the nation for his quick wit and intelligent views.

HUGH O'FLAHERTY

The Irish hero who saved
Jews from the Nazis

An Irish priest in German-occupied Rome during the Second World War led a double life to save thousands of Jews from the Nazi death camps. Monsignor Hugh O'Flaherty, whose exploits prompted several books and a film, also saved hundreds of prominent anti-Fascists, escaped prisoners of war and downed Allied bomber crews.

A Vatican diplomat who favoured the good life, he certainly seemed the most unlikely person to become a hero. He mixed in elite Roman society attending functions at embassies and the sumptuous villas of the rich and famous, and was a fan of the opera. He was also a keen golfer and raised eyebrows in the Vatican when he became the amateur golf champion of Italy!

But the Monsignor's easy-going lifestyle was to change

The man who ordered the deaths of millions.

for ever in 1942, when the Nazis took over Rome as the grip on power of Italy's Fascist dictator Mussolini began to slip. The Nazis rounded up the Jews and anti-Fascists. Monsignor O'Flaherty, who had socialised with many of these people before the war, now hid them in monasteries, convents and in his own Vatican residence – ironically the German College.

The Killarney, Co. Kerry-born Monsignor became known as an Irish Oskar Schindler – the German industrialist who helped thousands of Jews and others escape and whom Irish actor Liam Neeson brilliantly portrayed in the Hollywood film *Schindler's List.*

Monsignor O'Flaherty, who grew up in Killarney's Mangerton View, developed a network of safe houses

The film. Gregory Peck played O'Flaherty.

throughout Rome and planned escape routes into neutral Switzerland, risking his life for anyone who sought his help. Perhaps it was his initial experience of State terror in his youth which prompted him to act. While a seminarian in Ireland, some of his boyhood friends were killed by the dreaded British auxiliaries, the Black and Tans.

The Vatican and especially Pope Pius XII have been heavily criticised for not doing enough to fight Hitler's persecution of the Jews, but Monsignor O'Flaherty showed another side of the Church. He was the key figure in a European-wide Catholic network that saved thousands of Jews from the death camps. Monsignor O'Flaherty's group alone saved more than 5,000 of the 9,700 Jews of Rome from the horror of camps such as Auschwitz where 1,007 Roman Jews were murdered.

Early on in his clerical career, the Monsignor's undoubted abilities and Christian resolve had won papal approval. A bright scholar, O'Flaherty earned his bachelor's degree in theology in just one year at Rome's Urban College of the Congregation for the Propagation of the Faith. Ordained in 1925, he gained doctorates in divinity, canon law and philosophy and was appointed to the Vatican's diplomatic service. As the Nazi threat mounted, Pope Pius XII appointed Monsignor O'Flaherty as head of the Holy Office's intelligence gathering and humanitarian relief operation.

One historian said of O'Flaherty, 'Not for a moment did he consider staying quiet and doing nothing. Selflessly, he put his life at risk to stand up to the evil henchmen of Hitler's Nazi regime.'

The wartime pope: Pope Pius XII, he has been criticised for not
having done enough for the Jews of Europe during that time.

Hugh O'Flaherty as a young seminarian.

Every evening the man of God would stand in the porch of St Peter's Basilica and meet fleeing Jews and others seeking escape. He would sometimes make them dress in priest robes in order to get them to his safe houses.

The Nazis' secret police, the Gestapo, heard of the Monsignor's activities and targeted him for assassination and Pope Pius XII for imprisonment in the German monastery of Wartburg. They set up a spy network to trap him. On one occasion, when he arrived at a house to collect money to fund his operation, German soldiers suddenly burst in. The quick-thinking priest rushed to the basement, threw himself down a coal chute and, through providence, landed in a coal truck which was leaving the house and escaped capture. However, the noose around the saintly Irish Monsignor was tightening as his operations became more daring.

A definitive book on his life as a saviour of those hunted by the Nazis, *The Scarlet Pimpernel of the Vatican* by JP Gallagher, was turned into a film, *The Scarlet and the Black*, starring Gregory Peck, who bore a remarkable likeness to the Monsignor.

After the war, Rome's Gestapo boss Colonel Kappler, who ruthlessly hunted the priest, was imprisoned for life for his war crimes. But a forgiving Monsignor O'Flaherty was the evil Nazi's lone visitor in prison and, in 1959, baptised him.

After the war, the Monsignor was made a Notary of the Holy Office – the first Irishman to win the honour. He retired in 1960 and returned to live with his sister in Cahersiveen, Co. Kerry, where he died in 1963. Remembered by the Jews as one of their major saviours, he is also acknowledged in his native Co. Kerry. There is a monument in Killarney and, in the nearby national park at Muckross, a grove of 20 Italian trees – Cyprus holm oak, stone pine and Mediterranean palm – is dedicated to him. A plaque reads, 'To honour the Monsignor Hugh O'Flaherty (1898–1963). In Rome during World War II, he heroically served the cause of humanity.'

GREAT IRISH HERO
SEAMUS HEANEY

The poet and author was born in County Derry and studied at Queens University, Belfast. The natural successor to the great WB Yeats, Seamus has set the literary world alight. In 1995 he was awarded the Nobel Prize for Literature and he has also won the Whitbread book of the year award twice.

EDMOND J LANDERS

The Irish hero of the
Vietnam War

Historians helped to uncover the amazing bravery of an Irish fighting man in Vietnam. Survivors from Captain Edmond J Landers' 110-strong infantry troop told how he stood and fought overwhelming numbers of marauding Viet Cong. His courage enabled dozens of his men to escape the steamy jungle bloodbath by retreating to helicopters.

Edmond led men who destroyed 16 Viet Cong bunkers in the fire fight. The Limerick-born hero – a former barber's-shop boy from Oola – fought in hand-to-hand combat before he was caught in a hail of machine-gun crossfire.

His men formed the forward unit of an attacking force to stop thousands of Viet Cong and North Vietnamese troops advancing on Saigon. But wave after wave of

Captain Edmond Landers, proud in his uniform.

enemy artillery fire and mortar attacks halted the American advance.

Edmond, 29, died from appalling wounds. Seven of his men fell at his side. Six others were wounded.

The horrifying incident took up only minutes of the long, drawn out war which claimed more than two million lives from both sides. But it earned Edmond, the boy called Bunny by Irish schoolmates, the honour of becoming the most highly decorated Irish-born soldier fighting for America during the Vietnam conflict. One historian wrote of Edmond's exploits, 'He was a hero for Ireland and for America, and an inspiration to all Irishmen and women who serve peace and freedom.'

Soldiers in Vietnam, the most infamous war of the Cold War.

The shattering battle at Gia-Dinh, Saigon, on Sunday May 15, 1968, won Edmond the Silver Star for Gallantry in Action; the Bronze Star for Meritorious Achievements Against Hostile Forces from February to May, 1968; and the Purple Heart for Wounds Received in Action.

The news of Edmond's death was relayed to his wife Teresa, their three-year-old daughter

Chantelle and family by Oola parish priest Father O'Dwyer. A guard of honour escorted Edmond's coffin, draped in the Stars and Stripes, to the church cemetery. His medals were later presented to Teresa at the US embassy in Dublin. He is also commemorated on the Vietnam Veterans' Memorial in Washington DC. More than 4,500 men and women of Irish descent served in Vietnam with American forces and 21 are known to have

The soldier in his environment.

In action. Landers is third left.

been killed. The simple funeral service brought to a close the rich life of an Irish lad determined to do well.

Edmond was born in Oola in 1937, the youngest of a family of four boys and three girls. He spent 12 years at the local National School before taking his first job at a barber's shop in Main Street, Tipperary. His military life began at 18 when he joined the FCA in Oola at Sarsfield Barracks. He excelled and officers told him he was cut out for the rigours of army life.

Then at 20 he chose to change his life, in the way that thousands of other young Irish people had done, by emigrating to America. Initially, he lived with his sister in Napa, California, where he worked for the local power company. His tranquil life in the States did not last long, however. At 21, US military called him up for a two-year national service stint. Again, he took to the army life immediately and quickly gained the respect and admiration of his fellow soldiers. In Fort Bragg, North

211

Carolina, he earned his paratrooper badge and, after his two years, he knew he had found his calling and signed up for another three years.

The young soldier was getting to see the world, going to such exotic countries as Japan, and at the same time rapidly rising through the ranks, which was notoriously hard during peacetime. He reached the rank of captain, became an American citizen at Fort Bragg in 1963 and returned to his native land to marry his sweetheart Teresa in St Michael's Church, Oola, in 1964.

The couple spent a year in America before Edmond was posted to Germany. In 1965 the only child of the marriage, Chantelle, was born, but Edmond would have

Landers, centre, during his time at Fort Brigg.

Teresa and Chantelle Landers at the memorial.

little time to spend with her as a new posting of 12 months took him away from his family, who moved back to Tipperary to wait for his return.

In 1966 he was reassigned to Germany and was able to make frequent visits home to his family, but in 1967 the war drums were beginning to beat louder as America's involvement in Vietnam intensified. He was soon given his orders and told he would be shipped out to the war zone in early February.

In December, 1967, he returned to Tipperary to spend Christmas with his family and friends in the country of his birth. But little did they know that this would be the last time they would see him alive as he boarded the plane at Shannon Airport, heading for Saigon and the horrors of war.

213

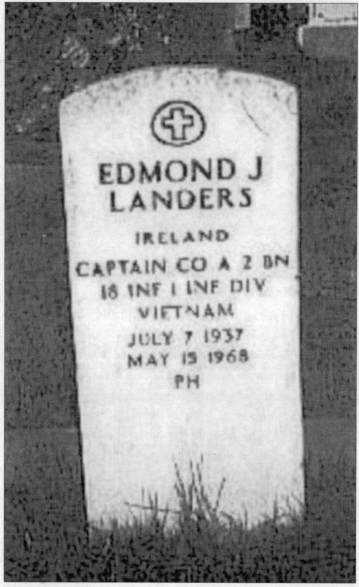

Captain Landers' grave.

He was quickly appointed commanding officer of a company stationed near Saigon, a unit that would see a lot of heavy fighting throughout the war. Then came the tragedy of Gia-Dinh. Edmond did not want his troops getting bogged down like a nearby stranded platoon. He quickly launched an operation to help them out as they were taking heavy casualties. When he reached the platoon with his own men he realised that he would have to make an assault on the enemy forces to fight his way out and save his men's lives.

Edmond bravely led them into battle but the position became hopeless. The heroic Irishman led the charge, running into a hail of bullets but managing to take a terrible toll on the enemy before he fell. He had begun to move towards a house, thinking that all enemy activity had ceased, when gunfire from the windows cut down the Irish soldier and his men.

His commanding officer wrote to his widow, 'I find it difficult to write to you as it reminds me of Ed and that black day of May 15. Not only did I lose an outstanding company commander, I also lost a friend along with several other fine soldiers.'

But the soldier was not forgotten and in 1999 at Ardare Manor in Co. Limerick – with the Taoiseach Bertie Ahern and Edmond's family in attendance – a memorial was dedicated to all the Irishmen who had died in the Vietnam War. The emotional ceremony was also dedicated to all the other Irish peacekeepers who had sacrificed their lives in trouble spots across the world.

GREAT IRISH HERO
THOMAS MACDONAGH

A poet, a professor and a revolutionary, MacDonagh was born in Cloughjordan. The son of a schoolteacher, he went on to become a university lecturer and a champion of the Irish language. In 1916 he signed the Proclamation of the Irish Republic, leading to his execution.

BILLY THE KID

How the Irish famine launched the legend of the Wild West's most notorious cowboy

Legendary bandit Billy the Kid would never have become the Wild West's most notorious cowboy had it not been for the Irish famine. The gun-toting outlaw went under the alias William Bonney, but his real name was Henry McCarty and his mother, Catherine, was Irish. She was born in Ireland in 1829, but was forced to flee in 1846 due to the raging famine that made thousands like her seek sanctuary across the Atlantic.

Alone and penniless, the 17-year-old arrived in America on board the passenger ship *Devonshire* on April 10, 1846. The teenager was now in a strange and alien land thousands of miles from her family and friends – she would never see them again.

For the next few years Catherine's life and whereabouts

Billy the Kid in his bandit outfit.

are disputed. What is known is that she gave birth to two sons, Joseph and then Henry. Life for her and most other settlers was tough. She lived on the streets and was forced to scrounge around in horrific conditions for food and money with her two children in tow. The brutal conditions took their toll on Catherine and she contracted tuberculosis. On the advice of doctors she moved her family out west. Little did she know that she was about to alter the course of American history.

The family moved to Indiana in 1866, where she met the man who would give her and her children a new surname – Antrim. The move was just what she needed and the following years were the happiest of her life.

Friends of the family would later recall how pleasant and full of life Billy the Kid's mother was. 'She could dance the highland fling better than most professional

218

dancers,' neighbour Louis Abraham said at the time. But for the new Mrs Antrim, even a fresh move to New Mexico where the climate was dryer could not save her from the inevitable. She died from TB aged just 45 with her boys at her bedside. On her deathbed she asked her friend and nurse Clara to take care of her two boys – but they were more than capable of looking after themselves.

Her obituary appeared in the morning paper Silver City Mining Life. It read, 'Died in Silver City – Catherine Antrim, wife of William Antrim. Mrs Antrim's health had not been good, she was suffering from a lung infection and had been bed-ridden for four and a half months.'

Without the guidance of his loving mother, impressionable teenager Billy soon found himself mixing with the worst elements in his neighbourhood. By the time he was 15, he had become a full-time criminal and was living up to his stepfather's prophecy that 'he was a little thief who was born to be bad.'

Just two years later Billy had earned his spurs and become a feared and leading figure in the criminal fraternity. He had been convicted of theft twice and had graduated to murder, gunning down the first of his 20 victims after a petty argument. Now a wanted man, he went on the run and began his reign of terror and murder.

In 1878, he famously shot dead a sheriff and his deputy in a land war between rival cattle ranchers in Lincoln County. He was captured but he somehow managed to escape jail along with the rest of his fearsome gang. The governor of the state then put a $500 price on his head – a colossal sum of money at the time. It was enough to

Dapper bandit Billy the Kid whose real name was Henry McCarty.

persuade former gang member and friend of Billy, Pat Garrett, to turn traitor. He took up the bounty and went out to hunt down the West's most infamous outlaw.

Garrett managed to track down his prey and arrest Billy and his gang after a three-day siege – but he was not behind bars for long. Billy escaped again. But this time he was convicted of murder and was sentenced to death in his absence. Billy the Kid had now become public enemy number one in America and he was running out of places to hide – his days were truly numbered.

The end came on the night of July 14, 1881, when Pat Garrett rode into the small town of Fort Summer on the trail of his former friend. When an unarmed Billy left his safe house that night to get some food, Garrett struck and shot him dead.

And so ended the short and violent life of Billy the Kid. He was just 22 years old. He may have been small and slight with tiny hands and feet and crooked teeth, but this son of an Irish settler left a brutal legacy that lives to this day. And even in death, his mother is remembered only for her son's deeds, for etched on her gravestone are the words, 'Here lies the mother of Billy the Kid'.

GREAT IRISH HERO
VERONICA GUERIN

In a career that spanned only six years, the crime-fighting journalist would leave an indelible mark on Irish life. Guerin received international recognition for her tireless crusade against Dublin's gangsters. However, she paid the ultimate price for her bravery when she was shot dead by masked assassins in 1996.

TEDDY ROOSEVELT

How President Teddy revelled in Irish roots

Tub-thumping US President Teddy Roosevelt spoke boldly of the old country long before the likes of Bill Clinton revealed their family ties. And his proud words lifted the hearts of tens of thousands of immigrant Irish. He gave them the strength for amazing endeavours by telling them the American dream was theirs.

'No one,' he cried, 'will again look down on you.' There was freedom and opportunity for the taking in their chosen land, he said, free of the yoke of oppression. The hero's blarney worked wonders for all immigrants, not just the Irish flooding into New York after cheap but rough sea crossings.

Theodore Roosevelt, the 26th President from 1901–09, whose mother's ancestors arrived from Lame, Co. Antrim,

John F Kennedy also boasted of his Irish connections.

Bill Clinton also has Irish roots.

in 1729, gave new excitement to the job. He spoke of having relations in Dublin, and he said, 'I am proud of every drop of Irish blood in my body.'

His high-pitched voice and arm-waving campaign antics caught the imagination. Teddy told the Irish the key to success was 'strenuous endeavour'. He said America could be a leading world power and his foreign policy axiom was 'Speak softly and carry a big stick.'

Historians are only now uncovering the story of the true debt Irish settlers owe to Roosevelt. One chronicler said, 'Long before John F Kennedy and Bill Clinton boasted of their Irish connections, Teddy Roosevelt became a hero to Irish settlers. He was the first American President to acknowledge his Irish roots – and the first Irish great hope in the US. He was a man of great principle who tried to change the unsophisticated image of the Irish and allow their culture to flourish.'

Teddy Roosevelt, the son of a rich New York family, became President at 42. As vice- president he took over when President John McKinley was assassinated. His first wife Alice had died in 1884 and he was heartbroken.

Teddy Roosevelt, when he was vice-president, with president
William McKinley.

His health failed and he spent two years as a cowboy on
cattle drives in the Badlands of Dakota to recover. He
even arrested an outlaw.

When he came to power it was not the done thing in
high political life in America to talk of immigrant links.
But he did. He helped set up a group called the American
Irish Historical Society to combat the Irish experience in
America being written out of history.

Teddy, once refused to shoot a tethered grizzly bear on
a hunt. It became known as Teddy's bear – and the Teddy
bear toy was born.

He left the presidency in 1909 but reappeared in 1912
running again for the top job. Then a fanatic fired a
single shot into his chest. But Teddy survived the attack in
Milwaukee and lived until 1919.

GRAINNE NI MHAILLE

The bald truth about
the pirate queen

A pirate queen who defied England and defeated the Royal Navy was once Ireland's most powerful woman. Grainne Ni Mhaille, the 16th-century beauty, was known to the English as Grace O'Malley and to her followers as Granuaile (Bald Grace) – a nickname she acquired as a young girl when she cropped her hair. She used the sea to carve out a life in which she defied Queen Elizabeth I, raided merchant ships off the west coast and humiliated Elizabeth's navy, winning many battles.

Born on Clare Island, which dominates Clew Bay off Westport, Co. Mayo, her many exploits on sea and land became legendary. Sir Richard Bingham, the English Governor of Connacht, described her as 'the nurse to all rebellions in the province for 40 years.'

Born in 1530, she inherited her ancestors' love of the

The powerful pirate queen.

sea – for 300 years the O'Malleys were renowned for their sailing prowess. Their galleys and three-masted carvals traded with Scotland, Spain and Portugal. The young Granuaile begged her father, Owen Dubhdarra (Black Oak) O'Malley – the elected chieftain of the Barony of Murrisk – to let her travel on one of his Spanish-bound ships. Her horrified mother told her that seafaring was not for a young lady. Defiantly, she cropped her black ringlets in a boy's style. Her amused family relented, allowing her to sail and thereafter called her Grainuaile – the short form of Grainne Mhaol.

The noble Granuaile married into another high-ranking family in 1546. Her husband Donal O'Flaherty had castles at Bunowen and Ballinshioch and was tainist, next in line to The O'Flaherty, chief of all west Connacht. They had three children: Owen, Murrough and Margaret. Granuaile gradually eclipsed her husband, becoming

The Irish coastline. The building on the left is Grainne's castle which still stands at Ballyytoohy on Clare Island.

more influential in trade and politics. When Connacht's capital Galway City closed its port and gates to the O'Flaherties during a trade war, it was Granuaile who took action. Her fast galleys patrolled Galway Bay to waylay slower merchant ships with their rich cargoes demanding 'a fair price' for safe passage. Any captain who refused had his ship plundered. Granuaile had become the pirate queen of Ireland and a thorn in England's side.

Granuaile's husband died during English-provoked inter-clan fighting with the neighbouring Joyces. But the pirate queen fought on, defeating her husband's foes and capturing their island castle. In 1556, to consolidate her rule over west Connacht, she married her nephew-in-law 'Iron' Richard Burke of Rockfleet Castle. They had a son, Tibbot, born during one of her trading voyages. The following day she was on the deck of her galley repulsing Turkish pirates. In 1558, Queen Elizabeth pardoned her in an effort to pacify the region but local English administrators continued their bid to subdue her.

In March, 1574, as her power continued to grow, the English sent a large fleet under Captain William Martin to deal with the upstart woman who was defying the Crown. The fleet besieged her in Rockfleet Castle for 18 days then she counter-attacked, scattering the fleet and winning a major victory.

Granuaile's piracy increased but her luck eventually ran out. She was captured while raiding the Limerick stronghold of the Earl of Desmond in 1577 and imprisoned for a year and a half in Dublin Castle. But she won her freedom after pledging her loyalty to the

Granualie 'bad Grace' drove off the English fleet which besieged her.

Crown, although she had no intention of keeping her pledge. In 1588 she was captured again and at one stage faced the hangman's noose. But she was released after 1,000 heads of her cattle, horses and other livestock were confiscated.

Having lost her livelihood on land and under constant harassment at sea, in 1593 she petitioned Queen Elizabeth, who had become enthralled by tales of the strong, bold Irish pirate 'queen'. Granuaile told Elizabeth that circumstances had 'constrained your highness's fond subject to take arms and by force to maintain herself and her people by sea and land the space of 40 years past.'

And, in a plea for a pardon for herself and her sons, she asked Elizabeth for 'free liberty to invade with sword and fire all your highness's enemies.'

Then Governor Bingham arrested her son Tibbot and brother Donal. Bravely, Granuaile sailed for London and, in a bold move, won an audience with Elizabeth. One court observer described Granuaile as a 'leader of men, seawoman without equal, pirate, trader, self-appointed ruler contrary to law and tradition but too powerful to be

The pillager and plunderer became a friend of the equally strong-willed Queen Elizabeth I.

dethroned, an elderly woman whose lined and weather-beaten face proclaimed the harsh conditions of her trade.'

We will never learn what was said between the two women in their private meeting, but it is known that Elizabeth welcomed the strong-willed woman as an equal. Granuaile won the freedom of her son and brother and was also granted a maintenance allowance after swearing allegiance.

Back home, she continued to pillage and plunder her neighbours but this time in the Queen's name.

Granuaile was in her 70s when she died peacefully in her sleep at Rockfleet Castle. At the time of her death the last of the Irish earls, Hugh O'Neill and Hugh O'Donnell, fled Ireland for Europe after their final defeat at the Battle of Kinsale in 1603. The Flight of the Earls, as it became known, ended the hopes of an Ireland free from English rule.

The legacy of Granuaile is still very much evident on the 4,053-acre Clare Island, which was once home to 1,600 people but now has a population of just over 100. Three buildings on the five-mile long, three-mile wide island are connected with Granuaile – the imposing four-storey castle where she grew up, a watchtower where she looked out to the Atlantic and the 12th-century Cistercian abbey where she is reputedly buried.

Carl O'Grady, owner of Clare Island's Bayview Hotel, said, 'She was the nearest thing Ireland had to Joan of Arc. These are daily reminders of her immense legacy – and this has had a positive effect on tourism. Even the ferry, the *Pirate Queen*, is named after her.'

GREAT IRISH HERO
ENYA

Enya is second only to U2 as the biggest-selling artist in Ireland's history. Born in County Donegal, the talented musician first hit the limelight in 1980 with Clannad. The group enjoyed huge success but she left in 1987 to launch a solo career. Her big break came a year later with the worldwide hit Orinoco Flow.